Somewhere Over the Sea

A Father's Letter to His Autistic Son

HALFDAN W. FREIHOW

Translated by Robert Ferguson

ANANSI

First published in Norway by Font Forlag AS
Published by agreement with Hagen Agency AS, Norway
First published by House of Anansi Press Inc. in 2007, under the title *Dear Gabriel*

This edition published in 2012 by
House of Anansi Press Inc.
110 Spadina Avenue, Suite 801
Toronto, ON, M5V 2K4
Tel. 416-363-4343
Fax 416-363-1017
www.houseofanansi.com

Distributed in Canada by
HarperCollins Canada Ltd.
1995 Markham Road
Scarborough, ON, M1B 5M8
Toll free tel. 1-800-387-0117

Distributed in the United States by
Publishers Group West
1700 Fourth Street
Berkeley, CA 94710
Toll free tel. 1-800-788-3123

House of Anansi Press is committed to protecting our natural environment. As part of our efforts, the interior of this book is printed on paper that contains 100% post-consumer recycled fibres, is acid-free, and is processed chlorine-free.

16 15 14 13 12   1 2 3 4 5

Library and Archives Canada Cataloguing in Publication

Freihow, Halfdan W.
Somewhere over the sea : a Father's letter to his autistic son / Halfdan
W. Freihow ; Robert Ferguson, translator.

Translation of: Kjære Gabriel.
Previous titles: Dear Gabriel : letter from a Father ; Dear Gabriel : letter
to an autistic son.
ISBN 978-1-77089-100-5

1. Freihow, Halfdan W. 2. Autistic children—Biography. 3. Parents of
autistic children—Biography. 4. Autistic children—Family relationships.
5. Fathers and sons—Biography. I. Ferguson, Robert II. Freihow, Halfdan
W. Dear Gabriel. III. Title.

RJ506.A9F7413 2012   618.92'85882   C2011-907010-3

Library of Congress Control Number: 2011940448

Cover design: Alysia Shewchuk
Text design and typesetting: Laura Brady

 Canada Council
for the Arts

Conseil des Arts
du Canada

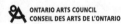 ONTARIO ARTS COUNCIL
CONSEIL DES ARTS DE L'ONTARIO

*We acknowledge for their financial support of our publishing program
the Canada Council for the Arts, the Ontario Arts Council, and the Government of Canada
through the Canada Book Fund.*

Printed and bound in Canada

 FSC
www.fsc.org

MIX
Paper from
responsible sources
FSC® C004071

 ANCIENT FOREST ™
FRIENDLY

SOMEWHERE OVER THE SEA

CHAPTER ONE

A seagull meditates on the ridge of the boathouse.

It stands out in grey and white against the moss, which is old, green and speckled brown with age. For fifty years now that clump of moss has clung on there, sheltered from the north wind, just to give colour and texture to the dull slabs on the roof. It's beautiful, and somewhere in the universe it probably makes sense.

Now the bird is done with its contemplating and dives down into the water, down to its secret supply of cold, wet food. Beyond that, I imagine, it has no plans.

The sea lies still today. It's sluggish, almost dead. The horizon stretches from sea to sky in a diffuse span that at times bewilders me. I know better who I am when sky and water are distinguishable, when there are limits and obstacles, when I know what is mine, when I can see where I belong.

It rained again last night, and I see the boat needs bailing out. And on the southern wall of the boathouse, the paint is flaking off, I see that too, where the rain streams, runs, holds on, doesn't whip as it does on the north side, peppering the wood with salt and brushing it to a hard, smooth gloss.

I'll bail out the boat. Today I'll bail out the boat. Come spring we should fix the boathouse.

I SIT HERE AND SEE all this from my study, Gabriel, all these things that happen just because they take place, because all things must find their place in order to happen. There are other landscapes, placeless landscapes where nothing happens, or where everything happens so fast and simultaneously that things become homeless in them. But here, in my study, I sit and I contemplate belonging. Not yours or mine, but a larger sense of belonging that invests this slow and patient landscape and enables us to lean against it as against a wall, though it's nothing more than air and water and the cry of seagulls, when our own vulnerable sense of belonging fails.

We need a wall at our backs, you and me. Sometimes a stroke from the palm of a hand is enough. At other times we need to erect huge edifices of insight and comprehension in order not to fall, plunge into bewilderment, foolishness, and fear. At times we are each other's wall, sometimes you are mine, but often I have to be yours alone, for you stumble and fall so easily. And sometimes that scares me, Gabriel, when I have nothing to hold on to myself, nothing to cling to, only wind and light and open sea, and you tumble beyond any comprehension.

WE DON'T TALK ABOUT any of this out in the garden, when you're home from school and the rabbits have been fed. Things like how fortunate we are to have each other and to live out here where the landscape is alive and tangible, we talk about only in our surplus moments, by the bedside when all is to be reconciled, or in the car, when glass and steel and high speed keep the world at bay. The good and the difficult each have their time, and we shouldn't confuse their moments. At home, after school, we need to concentrate on the usual, things we might as well have talked about yesterday without noticing any difference, and that's why we stroll across the lawn and chat about the animals, about what you want for Christmas, about what we'll have for supper. Conversing about things like this, things that effortlessly concern us both because they are down-to-earth and familiar, helps to maintain a level of control over these early evening hours that threaten to tear and burst now that there's no timetable to structure them, now that time doesn't have any place for us to be.

Then I might point to the boathouse and ask if you can see how worn out the roof looks. It's almost as though the ridge has a kind of fracture in the middle, I say, as though some heavy clouds have weighed down on it, or some very heavy air has been lying up there…

But your eyes reject this completely, and I realize that this was wrong.

— Air can't be heavy! Air weighs nothing, you say, half indignant at your father's ignorance, half afraid he might be joking, that this is a joke and that you therefore should be laughing.

You shake it off, don't pursue it. But a couple of hours later, as I'm clearing away the dinner table and we're waiting for children's TV to start, you still haven't forgotten.

— Yes but, Dad, why did you say there must have been some heavy air weighing down on the boathouse? Don't you know that clouds and air weigh nothing? Air is as light as anything! Here, look. And you lift up a handful, to demonstrate.

— Why did you say that, Dad?

— Well … I don't know … because.

I fumble and hesitate, for sometimes I need the small words, the seconds it takes to find an answer, to work out a strategy that will take your curiosity and confusion seriously without opening one of those endless why-discussions that don't get us anywhere, because you respond to all my answers with new questions.

— I was just joking, I say. Right then it's the best answer I can come up with.

— Just joking! It's not even true!

You no longer use your ordinary talking voice, you almost shout. I see in your eyes that you're unable to make sense of this conversation, that you feel wronged and that this might end very badly. You need help, but not humiliating help, to escort you out of the logical dead ends in which you fumble, confused to the point of hopelessness because you can't find the way out. You're not capable of reconciling an obvious absurdity, a lie, quite simply, with your instinctive belief that whatever Dad says must be true. And you are absolutely unable to entertain the possibility that you yourself are mistaken, have been mistaken for as long as you can remember, that air can in fact weigh so much that it threatens to break the roof of an entire boathouse. Paralyzed by a limitless need to feel safe, for assurance that the world makes sense, that everything has its ordained place in unbroken chains of cause and effect, that everything is as it usually is, you need a bridge, a hand to help you out of the labyrinth.

— But perhaps, I suggest, the beam in the roof is so old and rotten that it'll break under its own weight. What do you think? Should you and I go on an expedition to find out? Bring a torch and some hot chocolate to drink?

— It's not called that! You said it wrong!

I hear a loud edge of panic in your voice and rewind swiftly, reviewing my sentences in search of what it was I said wrong. It takes a few moments, but then I get it.

— Sorry, I didn't mean expedition, I meant *inspection*. You're quite right, we're not going off exploring, there's no treasure hidden in the boathouse, is there? What I meant was, let's take a torch and something to drink and go on an *inspection*, make sure everything's all right. Maybe we'll have to put on a whole new roof, what do you think?

You look at me with your very open eyes, just above and to the left of mine, a gaze so huge and at the same time so distant that I can't grasp it and don't know what it is you're seeing. I don't know whether you're still disappointed and a little afraid that I could lie and say that air is heavy, or if you hesitate because you're weighing up children's TV against an *inspection* trip to the boathouse, which is in such poor condition that you're not allowed to go in there alone, or whether you're simply someplace else. A place I cannot locate, a place where I can't reach you or know how you are, if everything hurts there or if nothing has any meaning, if you just take place there.

But then you roar out a huge YES! and throw your arms around my neck, and there's a presence in your eyes, a sudden accessibility, as though you've forgotten to be afraid, forgotten that you feel tricked, maybe even lied to. And then we do it, phone Mom at work to tell her what we're going to do, find the cocoa and heat the milk and butter the bread. That is, I phone and heat and butter. You watch, but I don't know whether you actually see, because once again you're someplace else, a place where only you know what happens.

WHEN A SEAGULL HAS FINISHED eating, what does it do? What does a full seagull do?

I don't have a clue. Perhaps it just flies away with its little seagull heart, heavy-bellied, and disappears somewhere over the sea. But one day it'll die, that I do know, and yet another unsolved life, another unanswered question will be added to the swarm of riddles that surround us, frame us and define us — the people, the animals, and our landscape, the astonishing powers that cause enormous trees to rise from tiny seeds.

I know many things, Gabriel. If I dig deep enough in my memory, I can even explain which laws of nature make it possible for thin, frail bird wings to carry heavily laden seagull bodies through the air. But most things I don't know, and the most important things I will perhaps never learn, even if I read an entire library.

And yet, every day, I tell you that the most important thing you can do is to learn. And I tell myself that the most important thing I can do for you is to help you and give you a desire to learn. When you one day read this, will you feel that I've tricked you, lied to you, as you felt I did about the boathouse roof? Perhaps you'll be a grown man yourself when you read these lines, perhaps you'll never bother. Perhaps you'll first lose me, and then the grief you never understood, and finally remember only the comfort and security with a man you called Dad, who promised you that everything would be all right, until you believed him because you didn't know any better, and because everything is better than despair. Perhaps.

Imagine that — I don't know who you are, I, who know you so well. I don't know what you remember, you who cannot forget.

THE BOAT CAN AT LEAST WAIT until tomorrow. And the boathouse that has endured gale-force winds, baking sunshine and sleet since before either of us were born, surely that can wait too? Until autumn maybe, or next year? Can't it all just wait, the washing-up and the reading practice and the children's TV?

I do not ask because I expect or suppose you have an answer to give me. I ask because I too am sometimes perplexed and consumed by doubt. I ask because I don't always know what is most important, because the large and the small become indistinguishable. I ask because time passes, but sometimes it stands completely still, and there are so many things I should have done with it. I ask because my love is strong and my grief is deep, and because they both take up so much space that I'm not quite sure what to do with them.

I ask because I see you, on a fine summer's day, sitting alone in the grass for an endless hour and studying a dandelion, yellow as egg yolk, and I don't know what you're thinking. I see your lips move as you minutely dissect the flower, but I don't know whether these are words, or what words you might be whispering. I don't even know if that's joy I see in your eyes, a small bliss, or if it's something else entirely. An urge to destroy, perhaps, to tear scrupulously apart? A need to expose the core of the flower, penetrate to its very heart? Or nothing, an emptiness that is not even absence of thought, not even flight from thought?

I ask because I once took you to the circus. You were eight years old and had been looking forward to it for days. You were dazzled, thrilled by the excitement, the lights, the colours, and the sounds. During the interval we bought candy floss and went around the back to see the animals, and you nagged me until you got a green light-sword, and then we returned to the high-flying trapeze artists and the trained elephants. After a while I saw that it was all getting to be too much for you. Gradually, you lost or abandoned your interest and sat there gazing down into your lap, or at the red light-sword belonging to the little girl in the next seat, even when I tried to make you look up at the dogs jumping through hoops of fire, or the flames spouting from the fakir's mouth. In the car on the way home I asked if you'd had a good time and you said it'd been fantastic. I asked you what you'd liked best, and you replied, without a moment's hesitation, the two clowns with the ball. I didn't respond then because I felt a sudden jolt of pain. There were, dear Gabriel, no clowns with a ball on the program that day. What you remembered best from your first experience of a circus was something that hadn't happened. The clown memory was probably something you'd picked up from TV, or overheard in some conversation about circuses at school. This is a kind of information you seem to archive automatically and probably unwittingly, to enable you to give a "correct" answer on some later occasion, in case anyone asks when your thoughts are occupied elsewhere, or in hibernation, or who knows where?

Your sister once said that if you wear glasses you have to take them off in order to describe them. She was quite right, and the same goes for people. No one can see themselves or understand themselves alone, without distance. Therefore I want to tell you about us, about our life, about the problems you face and that we are not always able to help you with. I will attempt to explain to you what is good, and what is difficult, and I shall see if I can put grief into words. I'll try to describe you, Gabriel, you and us, and our landscape. Maybe it'll help us to understand a bit more of where we are, and why, and who.

I have thought that this might be dangerous, for now and then it's possible to close one's eyes and hope that the hurt will be gone when one opens them again, and if I write about these things that will no longer be possible. It will be like revealing a secret. But then I have thought that there's really no point in keeping secrets alone, because in that case there's no one to talk to about them. And if there's no one to talk to about one's secrets, no one to share them with, it would be as if they didn't exist, and what are we to do with secrets that don't exist?

CHAPTER TWO

*T*rees don't grow where we live. They don't want to, I think, or they can't, our place is too exposed, the weather is too harsh. Trees are by nature slow and deliberate, they feel uncomfortable when there's noise and urgency and storms around them and they aren't left to grow in peace.

Out to sea, beyond the island where we've built our home on a little incline just a stone's throw from the water's edge, the North Atlantic lies open all the way to America. This naked landscape is no home for trees, hardly even for crooked, rusty bushes, heather, and peat. Farther inland, where the gusts of wind are not powerful enough to carry the salty ocean spray, where hills and small valleys, farms and settlements provide shelter, the trees gather in large and small huddles, like members of some silent, erect tribe. We visit them from time to time, the leaf tribe and the bark tribe, they live less than ten to fifteen minutes away, but that's already another world, one in which the sea sounds like a tall tale, a geography in which the coast's openness and overwhelming light are replaced by something that is closed and dark. For people who live out by the sea, the woods can seem cramped. A bit like in town, you know, where you often think it's difficult to find room for yourself.

But in the corner of our garden out by the sea, where south meets west, pressed up against the low fence, a lone tree stands and obstinately insists on its right to be a different tree. I don't know its name, or if there is a name at all for trees of this tenacious kind. I don't even know if you could say that it stands, at least not upright, in the way of trees. On one side of its trunk this tree is polished smooth by the wind, and it falls back, bows before the superior nor'westerly with a mixture of compliance and resolution that conveys great dignity.

All the branches point to the southeast. They strain and stretch, long and sinewy and horizontal in their flight from the wind. In winter, when the light disappears in the middle of the day and the branches are black and barren, they look like old, twisted witch's fingers grabbing at an eastern wind that won't be caught. In autumn, when the leaves are dry but have still not let go, they are wriggling tentacles, rattling snakes straining to break free of the firm hold of the trunk. In summer, when they bulge in green abundance and hum with birdsong and the murmur of insects, they are a lush, cooling bunch of self-enclosed, mystical life. And in spring, just before they burst into leaf, when they can but don't want to but must, they are pure longing, outstretched hands, refusal and will at one and the same impossible time.

Trees are bearers of big, ancient secrets, Gabriel. One should honour them as one honours the oldest and the very young, for without them one becomes rootless.

WHEN I SPEAK TO YOU about nature in this way, as though it had human feelings and thoughts, it's called anthropomorphism. Many think that anthropomorphism is inappropriate and should be avoided when one talks about nature, and in principle you would have agreed completely, for you don't like the mixing-together of things that don't belong together. But, in the case of our weather and our landscape, other rules apply. They are so intimately related to us that we easily forget ourselves and fall into conversation with them. It would seem strange to write to you about the nature around us as though it were not full of properties, and I think it would seem strange for you to read. We would both find it duller and less sociable than the one we deal with daily — less believable, almost.

Once, during a lengthy stay in hospital, you got tired of sitting in the ward all the time and announced that you wanted to go for a walk. Do you remember? It was windy and rainy, and the staff were resisting, but you insisted with an indisputable argument:

— But don't you see, I'm a child of nature?

And then the two of us went out into the rain, walked down to the pond, and fed the ducks and talked to them for a while.

THERE IS A CONNECTION between all things, Gabriel.

On the night you were born, February snow fell heavy over Oslo. It was six months before we moved out to the sea. Your mother, my Henni, had had a difficult pregnancy. You were her fourth, and the anticipation of at last meeting you was all the greater because we hoped that the birth would release not only you, but her too, from physical distress and worry.

As she lay in the delivery room and it was a matter of minutes rather than hours, the birth had been induced, I was called away. There was a telephone call for me in the duty room. At the other end, from another world in the west of the country,

I was told that your great-grandmother had passed away. Granny was dead.

I returned to the birth and could not say anything. Henni lay there surrounded by help but was alone in performing the miracle, in giving you life. When the midwife at last lifted you up and you opened your eyes and fixed them on me, limbs flailing as though you wanted to be nailed to life before you collapsed in weary exhaustion, it occurred to me that Granny was not dead in the irreplaceable sense of the word. She had, because her time was up and yours had come, yielded her place.

Only later, as we lay with your small, tired body between us on a waterbed in an adjoining room, did I tell your mother that her grandmother was gone, and we wept together. But the tears were not all bad. I think we both thought that one cannot always keep and at the same time get. It was a fine thought, strange and difficult.

Afterwards, as I wandered high on your birth through the fresh snow in the still of the Oslo night on my way home to your brothers and sister, I swear I saw a shooting star flash as Granny's soul set out toward that heaven she had always believed in so strongly and unshakeably and trustingly.

When you were six or seven years old and we told you about that night, about how your great-grandma died at the same time as you were born, you questioned us about her voice and her eyes. That's often your way of judging people, by listening to the timbre and pitch of their voice, by reading intentions and emotions in their looks. They can be angry, mean, or nice, and now you wanted to know if Granny had a nice voice and kind eyes. We told you as best we could about a wise woman with good hands and the very best pancakes. You reacted as so often before by asking for an expanded reply that would enable this new information to be incorporated into your own context, because it seems that you can only relate in a meaningful way to people you are able to regard as contributors or participants in your own life. Sometimes it's as though the others are little more to you than passing incidentals in the general distracting hubbub of life.

— Can Great-Grandma see that I feel like crying when I think about her? Will I get to meet her when I'm an old man and die and go to heaven? Even though I know that's a long time off?

The question was typical of you: despite the fact that it could only take place in the beyond, and a long time from now, you needed to establish a relationship on your own premises, within your own context, otherwise you would have had problems in distinguishing Granny from the rest of the hubbub.

We answered yes to your question, though we've no idea whether there is a heaven that welcomes the dead. We answered yes, because sometimes it's more important to preserve contexts than to tell the truth.

THE BEST WAY OF PRESERVING contexts is by remembering things that want to be remembered by us. That might seem a strange way to express it, but all I'm trying to say is that we select carefully the memories we store. Whether we make the selection ourselves, or whether it happens of itself as we encounter the world, isn't easy to say. Whatever, we cannot remember everything that is true, exactly what words were spoken, which shade of green the grass was in May. That is to ask for an impossible security. On the other hand, we can take memory cables and connect them to ourselves across dim chasms of time, and we can build bridges across great reaches of old, unknowable time by imagining the world as it offers itself to our memory. That way we ourselves can also be remembered, be incorporated by others into a sequence that is meaningful. The truth is intractable; it makes brutal sense like ice and steel, not soothing sense like contexts do, even though they may be untrue. Think of the tree in our garden — it carries not truth but stories of who you were when you climbed up and hid yourself in it, carved your name in it, dreamt of silver and golden treasures under it. The tree's roots are like channels through which your stories filter into other trees, other names, other stories. I imagine the trees holding the world together, Gabriel, holding it in an underground grip, a lattice of rooted fingers, and remembering for us. If you press your ear to the ground you can almost hear the stories murmuring in a chorus that obliterates yours and mine and sweeps us into all the others.

This is hard for you. For you, contexts can and must only be true, because you confuse them with logical structures, chains of cause and effect in which each link is unambiguous and inviolate. You have no faith in thoughts that develop from a flimsy base of possibilities, not even likelihoods. You dislike experiencing a mental progression that takes place in uncertainty, and you guard against building your own sense of belonging on the unreliable sense of belonging of others. Is that why you so often stand alone in a corner and reach out as though in longing toward the play of others, toward lightness of heart, but without taking part? Does it hurt so much to let go?

And yet no one has taught me better than you that there is a connection between all things.

You, apparently the least suitable of teachers. You who cannot, who dare not what the rest of us find exciting and challenging and demanding, all that is abrupt and sudden and unexpected, all that is breakup and change and transformation. You who even dislike surprises at home, at least when they're something other than presents, or news that we're going to do something we've done before that you know you like, and even then there had better be advance warning and plenty of time to prepare. Only such things as experience has accustomed you to — that you can expect small presents whenever Mom or

Dad comes home from a trip away, that broken things can be repaired or replaced, that stains can be washed out and wet clothes dried — only the unusual that has become usual because you've seen it happen so many times can you accept and appreciate without thorough preparation.

But most things in life are unusual, Gabriel, most things happen for the first time. Will you ever manage to come to terms with this?

MANY YEARS AGO, long before you were born, I took a parachuting course and was due to make my second jump. Mom was away at work or studying, and I had your sister with me. She must have been three or four years old. She watched wide-eyed as I stood in the enormous hangar and packed the parachute, guided by the more experienced jumpers, put it on, and was inspected by the instructors. I had arranged to have a woman at the jumping centre look after Victoria while I was in the air, and the three of us went out onto the runway.

I travelled a lot in those days, and Victoria often came along when Mom drove me to the airport. For your sister, there was an evident connection between accompanying Dad to a place where he boarded a plane, and the experience of him being away for several days, if not weeks. A long, long time in a little girl's world.

On this occasion she didn't have Mom there to comfort her when I left, only a kind but strange woman to whom I had entrusted her, holding her by the hand. When she realized that Dad had not only packed a weird backpack and dressed up in strange clothes, but that he was also going to board the waiting plane, that in other words he was leaving her, perhaps to stay away for a long, long time, and that she was going to be left behind with this woman whom she didn't know, she began to cry. On my way up the steps into the plane I turned and saw the silent despair in her eyes. It cut straight to my heart, so that I completely forgot to be afraid of the unnatural and unreasonable thing I was about to do — of my own free will throw myself out of a plane that was in perfectly good condition, several thousand metres up in the air.

It was probably only because fear had been displaced by a stronger impulse to comfort and hold my little Victoria, but I managed to guide the parachute almost directly down onto the marked landing site. Your sister stood there, obediently staring up into the air, following the minder's pointing finger. When she caught sight of me, when she saw that it was Dad, the one who had just disappeared into a plane to leave her, a light that I will never forget spread across her face. First naked disbelief, then pure shining happiness.

In the years that have passed since you came to us, I have many times thanked God it wasn't you who was with me that day. Had you been the child I suddenly abandoned in the care of a strange woman, only to reappear so suddenly and unexpectedly from the sky, you would have plummeted into a deep and painful crisis. It would have been impossible for you to adapt, to accept such a gross breach of your deep-seated need for contexts, for predictabilities, for time to grow accustomed — for things to be, as you put it, the way they usually are.

When you were the same age as Victoria was that day on the runway, Gabriel, it was even difficult for you to accept that you were served spaghetti for dinner instead of the meatballs we had talked about at breakfast. Even though you liked spaghetti a lot better.

YOU WHO HAVE TAUGHT me about contexts — not just how they simplify and make life easier and more comprehensible, but also how they add a reliability to life, a unique, rhythmic beauty that is the very foundation of long-lasting love — you are also more than any other the one who has astonished me.

Time after time I have thought: Good God, he's going to do it, he's breaking his own rules, he's daring to do the unplanned, the unprepared, he's deliberately seeking out that which is not as it usually is.

I'm not referring to occasions when you don't understand

social rules and conventions, like the time you stood behind me in the supermarket queue desperate to pass water, and were hurt and ashamed when I turned on you with anger in my voice because you had dropped your trousers to your ankles and stood there urinating in neat circles across the chocolate display. Or the time you walked out of the electrical goods store with Mom, your hands behind your back. She wondered why, and you proudly produced a portable CD player, exclaiming, when you saw her eyes darkening:

— Yes, but no one saw anything!

No, no one saw anything, Gabriel, but then neither had anyone explained to you that stealing is wrong even when no one sees you. You know quite well that you've done something you shouldn't have when someone finds out about it; but actions that are not discovered and reacted to, actions that go *unseen*, you somehow don't recognize as being fully real. Not even when they are good: I often suspect that you do not know, until someone tells you, that you've been kind or clever. It is often said of people like you that they live in their own, closed world, but that isn't quite true. To an even greater degree than others, perhaps, you discover yourself only in interaction. Without all the rest of us to reflect your actions and your individuality, you are alone in the loneliest sense of the word.

No, I don't mean these or any of a hundred other situations. We gave up dwelling on such scenes a long time ago. Mom and

I have since ceased to worry about scowling recriminations, vociferous complaints, rude accusations, nasty remarks ... about how ill-mannered you are, how impolite, what bad parents we must be ... poor child, imagine having a mother like that ... isn't it terrible the way some fathers neglect their children ... but, my dears, shouldn't he be in an institution?

Only on those occasions when bigger boys or adults let their ignorance affect you directly, on those rare occasions when they dare to hit you, or curse and threaten you, only then do I react, explosively, in furious outbursts that make most people back off. Then I feel, with an almost joyous fright, that I become dangerous, that I could hit, damage, and hurt. But most often we laugh it off, Mom and I, over a glass of wine in the evening. Over the years we have seen and heard so much insult, so many prejudices and ignorant remarks, that we've developed a kind of automated emotional response that enables us to transform them into good, funny stories.

And sometimes you are so pricelessly inappropriate that the laughter comes bubbling up by itself. On the way home from our holiday in Thailand, for example. It was late at night, and you staggered, drunk with sleeplessness and nausea, on board the Amsterdam plane, curly-haired, tanned, and beautiful as a little god, with your handpicked coconuts dangling from your fingers and a necklace of mauve orchids around your neck. We were on our way toward seat number forty-something at the rear of the plane when you came to a halt in the first-class cabin, looked around, caught sight of a glamorous model swathed in silk and sable two rows away, then resolutely marched over to her and vomited fourteen days' worth of ice cream, fizzy drinks, and fried rice all over her furs and Armani and bleached hair. A tactful and efficient air hostess sorted the situation out and you slept in my lap back there on seat 48F, and I stroked your head and thought Bravo! and laughed all the way to Europe.

BUT I DON'T MEAN any of this when I say you astonish me. Stories like these, which can be funny and sad, even both at the same time, are not about astonishment, about the enigmatic contexts that make you so different that science has found it necessary to make up new words for them.

CHAPTER THREE

— *I*s it true that God lives in heaven?

— Why does no one know God? After all, God knows all people. Has anyone ever seen God?

— God doesn't exist. He died a very long time ago. He died on a cross. Before that, God lived.

— Oh yes, God exists, I forgot, he came alive again. He didn't disappear and vanish forever.

— God must really be magic if he can make people appear on the earth. Otherwise how could he do it?

— No, God isn't magic. God isn't a human being at all. You once told me that.

— But how could God have been born into the world when he was the one who made it? Wait, no, that's it, it was Jesus who was born. But aren't Jesus and God the same?

YOU ASK AND YOU ASK, Gabriel, but God, Jesus, and heaven aren't things I know much about.

It's not surprising that you should want to know. At school they tell you stories from the Bible, you're taken along to church on various occasions, and many of the people who live in the area around us have a strong faith in God that can't help but influence you.

Whatever I've said to you when you ask, I've said carefully, because questions like these have to be approached with caution. They are difficult for all of us, and they are full of sinister verbal traps. It's never easy to know what people mean when they talk about God and heaven. They might mean it literally, that an old man with a white beard lives up there and that he once spent six days creating the world. They might also mean it metaphorically, that God is an idea, something that exists only in our heads. For you who are so infinitely literal in your understanding and interpretation of the world, it must be an almost insurmountable trial to keep check of such multifarious concepts for which you have no tangible frame of reference.

You have an impressively large vocabulary, which you employ with exquisite precision. But in your sentences everything has to have its ordained and regular place, because you are dependent on words having and imparting a single, clear, and unambiguous meaning. You'll only smile condescendingly if, for example, we ask you to "hold your horses," or explain that in order to make bread you have to "knead" the dough. And if someone asks you, when it is obvious that your hair is a little shorter, if you've cut your hair, you answer with friendly exasperation:

— No, I haven't cut my hair. I've been to the barber's.

There are certain expressions you've learned to accept, even though you probably think of them as being woefully imprecise. I remember well when you were smaller and I asked you, for example, if you could pass me the milk. "Yes," you said, but without doing anything with the milk carton, because to your ears all I had done was ask if you were capable of passing it to me.

Now you are able to understand that certain questions like this can have an implied meaning, and you act accordingly, passing me the milk without requiring a specific request to do so. But you neither understand nor see the point of most linguistic oddities and tools — irony, satire, jokes, double entendres, sarcasm, and metaphor. To your ears they only serve to create distorted meaning, misunderstanding, and disorder. How to explain to you things like faith and sin, resurrection, and redemption? And, moreover, how to explain that these words, which you (and all the rest of us!) have such difficulties in understanding to begin with, have different meanings within different religions, and even for different people within the individual religions? And how to explain to you that for some other people these words don't mean anything at all, without that necessarily making them stupid or bad?

Then I choose, as I perhaps too often do, the simplest solution. All people are different, I say. Some believe in God, some in Allah, some in Buddha. Some others don't believe in any of them, and many people don't know what to believe. Me, for example. I don't know whether it was God who created nature, or whether nature created itself. I don't believe we go to heaven when we die, but I don't know. Nor do I know whether there is a hell where we will be punished for our sins, but I choose not to believe it.

THINKING AND KNOWING are two very different things. You have understood that. Often, when you ask me a question that seems difficult to answer, I will say:

— I don't know.

You don't like to hear that, so you immediately follow up:

— But what do you *think*? Do you think it's true that the sun will explode?

— Yes, but in a very, very long time.

— Do you think I'll be in heaven by then?

— Yes.

— Do you think the angels and gods and so on can arrange for heaven not to catch fire?

— ...

You want an answer. That's to say, I suspect you want confirmation of the fact that there is always an answer, regardless of what it might be. The content of the answer is often subordinate; above all you want to know that all questions have their answer. Because if there is not one — and only *one* — answer to each individual question, then how can the world make sense? How are you supposed to relate to a world that lacks answers?

You have no choice, son. I don't want to make things more difficult for you than they already are, but there is no way around it. Just as you have to live with the fact that all people know and believe and think in different ways about different things, and as a result there is no formula you can learn to tell you what a person is and you will have to accept that you will never get answers to everything, that very often there is no answer, no matter how hard you search, and that there will always be more questions than answers. Even for those who believe in God — that's precisely what they do — they believe.

To believe can mean several things. It can mean imagining something you cannot know, as when you *believe* that you'll be an astronaut when you grow up. It can also mean to trust, as when you say you have been given and not taken a marble at school, and I say that I *believe* you. And it can mean that something is likely, but not certain, as when I *believe* that Victoria will be angry if you go rummaging through her things. And then it can mean a mixture of all of these — to trust in something one cannot know but that seems likely. Perhaps it's something like that people mean when they say they believe in God.

I know this confuses you. First I tell you that you will never get answers to all your questions, because sometimes there just is no answer. Then I tell you that it isn't all that easy to believe either, since it's possible to believe in so many different ways that you don't know what to believe, or how.

So let's forget them for a moment, both the believing and the knowing. Let's instead think another thought. Let's pretend that the world is one enormous church, or a huge temple. You know what I mean, you like being in churches and temples. Let's suppose that every place in the world — every country and city and river and mountain and volcano and forest and sea and desert and jungle — that all of these places are inside a church that is as big as the whole earth. And that all of the life in all these places, everything that grows and breathes and crawls and walks and flies and swims, lives inside this temple that is so big that nothing can manage to survey it — not the animals, not the plants, not the birds, and not the fish. Not even the humans.

Because it isn't always necessary to survey, to understand. Sometimes all that is necessary is to accept. Sometimes it's necessary to do as you said to me once when I wanted to talk to you about something you thought was unpleasant:

— Can't you just think that thought away?

You were quite right. It took a while for me to understand, but it was wisely said; I understood that later. Sometimes you have to think your thoughts away, otherwise you'll just feel sad, or perhaps angry, or perhaps even a little crazy. As when you ask me why it isn't possible to make gold, or why Victoria was born before you, or why it isn't warm enough to sunbathe in spring, and I say that's just how things are. That is an answer you dislike, because you want everything to have an explanation. And yet now and then I can see in your eyes, in the tension that seems to let go, first from your shoulders and then your whole body, that you manage it — you think the thought away, and it does you good.

When I sit in a church, or a temple, I let go. I like it. I like to feel that here, in this building that is called holy, it is safe not to know what is true and what is a lie. Normally, at work, or at school, or at home, or in the shop, we have to think all the time about what is right and what is wrong. We have to know all the time, and always be in a position to explain why and how we know. But in a church you don't have to know. There you don't even have to believe anything at all. Perhaps it's because God is in there, and he is so mighty and wise that it doesn't help anyway to think your own small, human thoughts. Or perhaps not. I don't think it's all that important whether God exists or not. But there is something about these buildings that feels good, that brings peace and consolation and a calm joy — because in there it's possible to give up the need to know and instead be filled with a strange and good desire to give thanks and to enjoy.

Imagine then if the *whole* world were a church, or a temple. Then we could be anywhere — in Africa, on the beach, at home — and still find consolation and security. If everything that exists in nature, plants and water and stones and air, and everything that mankind has built and created — if everything were a church where you were allowed not to understand, not to believe and think, then we would be secure wherever we went.

You had a similar idea once yourself, when you were about to go on your first class outing and spend the night in an unfamiliar forest and were a bit anxious. Mom and I said we could come with you, but you protested:

— I don't need any grown-ups with me. Jesus can look after me; he can even walk on the water!

And then you added, just to be on the safe side:

— But perhaps you could ask him to take God and Buddha with him too? And the other one, what's his name, Anna?

YOUR NEED FOR unambiguity and literal meaning can often seem unreasonable to others, but they are counterbalanced by some exceptional qualities: you are profoundly honest, sincere, loving, and fearless. These qualities are so highly characteristic of you that it's almost more correct to say that they *are* you. They form your natural, congenital defences. Without them you would have been... I hardly dare think the thought.

But these qualities are not something you have chosen to develop. They are not part of a strategy you've worked out in order to succeed or to be liked. You, who are so talented, are incapable of strategic thinking. It goes against your nature, against that part of your nature that does not understand that in their dealings most people act as if in a game, with unwritten rules that seem to be there to be broken, but not always... a system of changing conventions, dictated by circumstance, which is incomprehensible to you and therefore impenetrable.

If it were the case that you had consciously chosen to oppose this game, which can often seem so petty, but which most people nevertheless use when they deal with others — if it were the case that you consciously chose to reject it and instead face the world with an unconditional openness, you would have been courageous in the sense of daring and foolhardy.

But that's not the way it is. You have simply been given no choice. You know of no other way in which to relate to people; you lack the ability to dissimulate and to understand that there might be another way. It makes you vulnerable in a way most people find inconceivable. Moreover, it makes you what people call *difficult*, because the others don't always know how to answer you, they don't understand you, they are unable to escape the suspicion that you are the one who is playing with them, that you, the child, have an inexplicable and intolerable advantage over them, and that you must be overcome as a matter of urgency, if necessary by means of the most dirty and brutal tricks in the game.

Nevertheless, these qualities make you, above all, a great and fine person, Gabriel. An enrichment for those of us who know you, and a corrective. They make it a privilege to learn from you and a joy to educate — in everything that can help you to live with your own vulnerability and the bewilderment of others, everything that can shield and strengthen your own experience of happiness.

Ever since you began asking us about your difficulties, those things about yourself that seemed different to other people, your knotted thoughts, we have given them the name "problems."

You use the word yourself too, sometimes in a way that may seem cunning and calculated, when you're caught doing something you know you're not supposed to:

— Oh yes, sorry, but you know me, I've got some problems.

But that happens only rarely. Usually you convey a profound distress when you talk about your problems, for behind this everyday word lie great and fathomless riddles like the frightening mysteries of the deep — the enigmatic reasons why you are not like others.

You have several times asked us if we're going to "fix" your problems. Without your having to explain the question we've understood that what you have in mind is some kind of cure, an unvoiced expectation that Mom and Dad will make your problems disappear. But, dear Gabriel, however much we might wish to, we cannot.

Of course we'll do all we can to help you, but even though we're both adults as well as your parents, we don't in fact know all that much about what we can and should do. We know what we have read and what we've been told by the health authorities and pedagogues and therapists, but often they don't even agree with one another. Some, for example, think that a change in diet would have a beneficial effect; others suggest we use special methods of training to change what they call "undesirable behaviour"; still others maintain that medication is the answer.

What makes all these options so difficult and unreliable is that every child with problems like yours is unique and different from every other. So a method that achieves good results in one case won't work, or works counterproductively, in another. And no one can know in advance who will react positively, or negatively, or not at all. All parents must therefore make some difficult decisions about which piece of advice to heed. Are they to expose their child to the endless burden of trying out one theory after another? It's almost like sitting in a restaurant with a menu full of dishes you've never heard of, and having to eat them all one after the other, but not knowing whether you're going to like or tolerate any of them.

You discovered for yourself how difficult it is when we took you to stay for a month in hospital to try out medications. Even though the doctors assured us they worked on the majority of children, they did not work on you, or else had a clearly negative effect. You lay awake at night, and finally got up, found crayons and a sheet of paper, and drew a round stomach with a long coiled intestine in it. Inside the intestine you put a tablet, drew a big red cross over it and said:

— I don't want any more of these tablets that glide through my stomach. I can't sleep. I'm not dreaming, but I'm inside a nightmare and my head's going around. Get rid of these medicines!

No, Gabriel, we don't actually know much more about your problems and what to do about them than what you've taught us, and what we've understood from being your parents. On this flimsy basis we've made our choices and taken our chances. We have, for example, chosen not to embrace complicated and demanding theories about nutrition and diet — quite simply because it seemed to us that the minute scrutiny of the contents of every sandwich you eat, every sweet, every sauce, and piece of cake you might come across, would be unreasonably demanding when weighed against the possible but highly uncertain potential benefits.

Our choices are guided by two wishes we have for you: that you will live, as much as possible, a life of equal status with other people, and that you will have as many chances as possible to know what you yourself call happiness. We resist methods of treatment that risk sidelining you and increasing the feeling of being different that you already have. So instead we usually turn to what seems most natural to us: showering you with security and praise and love.

We're proud of you, son, and proud to be your parents, just as I know your brothers and sisters are proud to have you as a brother. Never doubt that, not even when our helplessness and doubt seem to you like betrayal. Because we too can be foolish and hurt you, forget that you're not an ordinary piece in the people game. That is another task we face, to teach you, even though it might hurt, that even your own family and friends, those whom you most trust, can be weak, stupid, and unfair, too self-centred to make allowances and approach you the way you wish to be approached.

One warm summer's day I lay out sleeping in the hot sun on our skerries. You snuck up on me with a bucket full of cold sea water and emptied it over me. I leapt up, extremely annoyed and probably glowering at you. You looked at me in a kind of naked wonder and said, almost disbelievingly:

— But, Dad, you wouldn't hit your own son, would you?

Of course not, son. But how is it that you're so often ahead of me with your fearless sincerity?

ON RARE OCCASIONS you happen to meet people who see and somehow recognize you. And you do the same, in a strange, intuitive reciprocation. As a witness on such occasions, I can only assume that a bridge of spirituality spontaneously spans the two of you, although spirituality is something I normally shrink from in skeptical distrust. But the choice is not always mine, for you have also taught me about veiled contexts, Gabriel.

For example, we visit a Buddhist temple on an island in Thailand. In the library at home I have a large bronze Buddha that has always fascinated you — to such an extent that the prospect of acquiring one yourself for a long time was your main motivation for fussing about when we could travel to Thailand. Now we're off to the temple where I bought the figurine all those years ago, and your whole being radiates with the solemnity of the occasion.

The first thing you see, long before we're inside the temple walls, is the enormous gilded Buddha statue atop a pyramidal structure. It must be at least twenty to thirty metres high, and it stares, with blind inscrutability, through eons and universes. As soon as we're out of the car, and without a prompting word from either of us, you remove your sandals. Then you head off up the steep stairway that ends at the feet of the statue. The decorative railings on either side are shaped like slender, coiled bodies of dragons. I follow and catch up with you at the top, where you have already lost interest in the colossal dispenser of wisdom. What interests you now is the peeling gold flake: Is it real? How can I say there's such poverty in Thailand when they have this much gold? Aren't the monks, at least, very rich?

You seem uninterested in the flowers and the incense, the wreaths and the bowls containing offerings of food in front of the small altars. You make a kind of dutiful sound, tapping half-heartedly with a hollow stick on the bells and cymbals hanging from the framework of beams around the statue to produce the primordial sound *o m*. You disregard the panoramic view. You want to go down again to buy your own Buddha.

We locate the temple's sales booth and, after some agonizing, you make your choice: not the largest, not the most expensive, not even one made of bronze. You want the medium-sized one cast in stone, light beige, with a reddish glint — as long as we can assure you that it's made of a genuine, that's to say, a precious type of stone.

The purchase made, you want to leave. It's hot and you want to get back to the beach. Moreover, the temple evidently doesn't live up to your expectations: the monks' cells are low, grey concrete blocks, and there are no glinting and glittering treasures. You're pleased with your statue, but otherwise disappointed — this place has nothing to do with the temple splendours we've seen in pictures of Bangkok.

While you hurry off toward the exit, I turn to gather the rest of our party. It takes only a moment to signal that we're on our way out, but when I turn back, you're gone. From the gateway I peer out over the parking lot but see no sign of you. I'm about to go back in again, thinking that perhaps you've managed to slip past behind me and return to the statue, when I see you.

You stand facing a kind of enclosure that lies half hidden between large green plants in enormous pots, beneath the dense crown of a tree through which sunlight doesn't penetrate. I approach closer and see, beyond the interlacing leaves, half a step down, a beautiful silk rug, like a processional runner. It leads to a low, carved bench, almost a little throne. An ageless monk sits there, cross-legged, shaven-headed, and swathed in orange. There is something inexpressibly mild about his face, and in the eyes that twinkle at the world and past it through simple, round glasses. It occurs to me at once that he must be the head of the monastery.

You stand quite still, as though waiting. There are ten metres between you.

Then he makes a tiny movement of the head, a fraction of a nod, hardly more than what follows from a wink. You remove your T-shirt, sandals, and cap, lay them to one side, and approach him along the rug. When only a couple of metres separate you, you slowly sink to your knees and bend your whole body forward, until your forehead touches the silk. There you lie in what seems to be pure, devoted submission.

The slightly built monk turns slowly to one side, dips a long-handled brass bowl into a jar, and fills it with water. Then he lifts it, reaches out toward you, and splashes the water over your head and down your back, muttering and chanting something that can only be a blessing. You do not move a single muscle as the water touches you. You lie there, trusting, and knowing, with a knowledge that is closed to me.

Afterwards you stand up, cast a quick glance at the monk, pick up your shirt, sandals, and cap, and ask if we can leave soon. The small, modest man has closed his eyes and is gone somewhere behind the foliage of illusion.

Later that day we build a pyramid of sand on the beach, carefully carve out the steps, shape coiling dragons' bodies with wet sand, and place your Buddha on top. I try to ask you about the monk, but your eyes tell me that you don't want to or can't answer.

It's already evening when it happens, just as you're about to go to bed. All of a sudden you conjure up a furious anger. You rage and curse at that stupid monk who threw water on you. I don't know what has happened; I only understand that the frail web of trust you two spun together earlier in the day has, for some reason or other, disappeared. In its place there is now only profound indignation and angry reproach.

But ten months later, one evening at home by the bedside, you suddenly exclaim:

— Oh, Dad, I love your dream!

I don't quite know what to say to this, and a long silence follows.

Then you ask:

— Dad, what exactly is your dream?

— Well . . . to be good and kind, and help others, I reply rather vaguely, caught off guard.

— So what's your dream then, Gabriel?

You think for a long time.

— To be rich! In money and treasures, I mean. But also in love.

I still don't know what to say, and you lie looking up at the ceiling a while before you continue.

— Because I'm actually just like a monk. Only I collect treasures and of course monks don't. But otherwise I'm just like a monk. A Buddhist monk, I think.

CHAPTER FOUR

*T*oday I'll have to bail out the boat after all. Not from any sudden manifestation of a sense of duty, but simply because the sun is shining. Out here by the sea most things have to give way when the sun shines, even our reluctance to perform practical tasks that should have been completed long ago.

The sun is shining, despite the fact that it is October, and from the north a breeze blows, temperate and caressing. I don't know where the clouds have gone to, but it doesn't really matter, because they aren't here. This morning, when you and Victoria and Mom left for school and work, the sky hung low in shades of grey, drying out after the night's downpour. But over the last few hours it has retreated upward again, higher and higher, until the cloud cover lost its grip and had to find another and lower sky to attach itself to, perhaps over Bergen, that's not my problem. Here, at any rate, the sun is shining as though that's all it had ever done, you'll be home in an hour and a half, and I must bail out the boat because we need it.

Balder realizes at once what's about to happen when I descend the steps to the cellar, find my wellington boots and pull on the green anorak. Balder's father was a cocker spaniel, his mother a mixture of border collie and beagle, and you won't find a better pedigree anywhere. You and he were born within a few months of each other and have grown up together, although as a dog he's getting on a bit now. He's black as night, has a good temperament, is loving and loyal, and I've no doubt at all that in his own quiet dog-mind he considers you his best friend. Balder's only failing is as a watchdog: whether it's me driving up or Victoria on her bicycle, he gives the same two or three half barks as he would if the house were surrounded by bloodthirsty terrorists. On the other hand — if we haven't got any clothes on, we always manage to get dressed in time when Balder announces an approach.

On the lawn outside the cellar door I stand still a moment. I often do. It's not because the grass reminds me of yet another long-postponed task, but because this vantage point is the site of an early memory of you that gradually has become one of my saddest. You couldn't have been more than six months old. We had just moved here from Oslo, it was an evening at the height of summer, and I stood out here on the lawn with you in my arms beside what was then the henhouse. Together we admired the view, as one contemplates a newly conquered kingdom: emerald-green pastures tumbled down toward the shore; the sea glinted in copper and amber and ruby red; islands were black velvet rimmed in gold, the horizon a treasure chest, and the sky an ineffable immensity of sapphire blue.

Perhaps it was on a whim, but it felt like a certainty. I lifted your little hand in mine to point, turned in a slow, sweeping circle and said:

— This is your home, this is yours, here is where you will live, Gabriel.

At the time it seemed logical: your oldest brother, Kai Henrik, had already moved out before we left Oslo. He was about to find his own place in the world, and as the first-born he would inherit a building plot. Alexander, the next oldest, was so uncompromisingly headed into his teens and everything that didn't have to do with a life in the country in the parental home that it seemed out of the question he might ever want to settle here. Victoria was aged seven and had already given every indication of having abilities and qualities that would take her far; she would be needing things very different than a house by the sea. That left only you, the last-born, to be raised by wind and sun, to grow into the landscape and one day take over. Or so I thought. It was a good thought, for it vaulted continuity over our little moment on the lawn, as the fairy-tale landscape shimmered everywhere around us.

Three years later it was with a very different kind of certainty, a new and painful knowledge, a so-called "diagnosis," that I had to picture your life here. A life to which you suddenly seemed condemned, a life you could not reject, nor were capable of rejecting. Since then few months have passed without you asking, with a kind of mantric need for confirmation:

— Can you promise me, Dad, that I'll always be able to live here?

TODAY, HOWEVER, THE SUN shines from a spotless sky, and no doubt there's a gale blowing in Oslo, but I don't think about that, for I have a boat to bail out. Balder and I follow the track down to the boathouse, which is only used by the sheep and those of us who live here. Not only because of the weather, but on account of the sheep too, we will one day — in the fullness of time — have to fix the boathouse. In the summer they like to seek out the shade on the northerly side, but the paved path along the wall is so narrow that they're forced to scour their rough wool against the woodwork, in a trade-off that removes flaking paint and leaves muck behind.

The hell with it, I think as I round the corner and step onto the jetty. At least what it pleases us to call a jetty; it is possible, at high tide, to lie alongside there.

The boat — which you like to call a ship, or a vessel, because who's ever heard of pirates in a boat? — is a sorry sight. The water inside and the water outside are almost on a level. It takes all my strength to drag it close, and a talent for balance I don't even know I have to keep my footing on the thwarts while I fill the sea, bucket by bucket, with fresh quantities of new water.

It takes an hour, even though we're talking about a fairly modest fourteen-foot ship.

I leave it to the sun to sip up the last drops and hardly dare to believe it when the motor makes a promising sound on the third attempt and starts on the sixth. Then I go ashore with a "No, not yet, Balder" to the tail-wagging enthusiast on the jetty, and fetch the blankets and foam mats and life jackets we're going to need. Then I hurry up to the house, which you like to call a castle, or a fortress, because kings and princes don't live in ordinary houses, do they?

Victoria lies half asleep on the sofa in front of the television. She doesn't want to come; she's waiting for her boyfriend. Apparently the same one as yesterday and the day before, so it's probably serious. Mom has a meeting straight after work and won't be coming until later.

In the fridge I find the chops I was hoping for, and even a bottle of white wine behind the vegetables. Into the cooler with them, along with the freezer elements, juice, a bar of chocolate, and the vanilla yogourt that was actually saved for school tomorrow. No need for water for Balder, he manages well enough with what he finds in puddles and cracks in the rocks. Into a plastic bag I put a roll of kitchen paper, cutlery, marinade, glasses, a corkscrew, paper plates, and two Thermoses, one with coffee and one with cocoa. I'm standing there thinking that the charcoal and the white spirit are in the shed when Balder announces an arrival. Through the kitchen window I can see that it is your taxi.

I wouldn't say a word against the council's taxi service that makes sure you're conveyed to and from school each day. It's a generous service, I think, and not something I should take for granted. I also understand that the council has to save money, or that the council's money has to be saved, or whatever. All the same, it gives me a little jab to the heart each day when the maxi-taxi drives up, mornings and afternoons. It's cheaper this way, they say, and I understand that too, but I don't like it, see-ing you rounded up in the bus for pupils with special difficul-ties, along with multi-handicapped children who sit chained to their wheelchairs and are hardly able to communicate with their surroundings. Let them call it what they will — demanding, inappropriate pride — but I don't like it, for I can't help asking myself what you think. You rarely say anything, but do these daily drives in the company of those who are so much less endowed than you have any influence on your self-image? Are you gradually being driven to see yourself as you see them? Have you heard what the others at school call it, the spaz-taxi? Does that bother you? Do you find it hard and hurtful to talk about? One day they told us at school that you had pulled some poor girl's hair and tried to tip her wheelchair over, because "she makes a mess when she eats and she can't speak." Was it your own hair you were pulling, Gabriel?

But like I said: praise be to the council's taxi service, we'd never have managed without it, and today the sun is shining and it's a bright little lark of a boy who comes running to greet me.

— Hi, Gabriel, how good to see you!

I open my arms to receive you, but you have neither the time nor the capacity for such attention:

— Yeah, yeah, I know, let's not talk about it anymore. Do you know what Morten told me today?

I don't know who Morten is and answer only:

— Morten at school? No, what did he say?

— That I might, just *might*, get a genuine, a real *genuine* lump of gold from him! Isn't that fantastic?

You're bubbling so much it's difficult to get through to you.

— Yes, that's really fantastic. We'll just have to wait and see what comes of it, because genuine gold lumps are very expensive, you know. But do you know what? Today...?

And then I tell you what I've planned, sneak in fragments of sentences about boat trip and barbecuing and juice and chops every time you stop to draw your breath between identical-sounding repetitions of how fantastic it is that you *might* get a real *genuine* lump of gold from Morten.

In the end we're agreed: we'll have to wait and see. Now let's go to sea.

THERE'S BOUND TO BE an optimal logistical order in which to do these things, but I've never found it.

You and Balder both hop about impatiently on the edge of the jetty and want to get into the boat, but neither of you understands that you're in the way — that I've got blankets and foam mattresses and cooler and plastic bag and charcoal to load, that there's a bow I've got to hold close enough to the jetty to be able to reach out for all this between your legs, but not closer, otherwise it'll get roughed up against the concrete, that there's a life jacket I've got to help you into while doing the splits, with one foot on the edge of the jetty, the other on the bow, and a motor that for God's sake mustn't overchoke and flood, otherwise it'll stop, and a flooded carburetor in an outboard motor is a nightmare.

But everything works out fine. The gear and the dog are on board, the motor is ticking over nicely, all that remains is to fold out your blanket at the forward end of the boat, and then it's your turn. I've cast off fore and aft and I'm holding on to the jetty with one hand and with the other helping you step aboard. You move one foot down into the boat, stand with the other still on the jetty, and then you stop. You stare out into space, as though rehearsing something, and then you turn to me and say, completely oblivious to our current situation, as though we were sitting in the living room and not halfway through a delicate manoeuvre between land and sea:

— Dad, why is it actually so fantastic that I might get a lump of real gold from Morten?

— Just get into the boat! I've no idea! Do as I tell you!

It all comes out much harsher and dismissive than I intend or actually feel, but honestly.

— Yes but, Dad, why…

— Gabriel!

This time my voice leaves no room for doubt. Fortunately, you take the hint, put your other foot on board and get yourself seated comfortably. I breathe a sigh of relief, let go of the edge of the jetty, hurry aft to the motor before the current drifts us into even shallower waters, throttle out into the sound, and am about to light a cigarette, which seems to me deserved.

The grill! I've forgotten the grill for the barbecue! Not much use in charcoal and white spirit and chops without a grill. As far as I can recall, it's in the shed.

About face and in again. I explain to you what it is I've forgotten, that I must go up to the house to fetch the grill, and ask if you're sure you can sit there quietly and wait for me.

— Shall I bring some toys for you while I'm at it? Some treasures, maybe?

I ask not only to be nice, but also because doing an errand for you gives a somewhat greater legitimacy to this annoying little extra trip. You explain in detail what you want and where you *think* it is, and promise not to go anywhere or get into trouble while I'm gone.

I'm still irritated by my own forgetfulness as I stomp back up toward the house; but then for a moment I contemplate that it's probably pouring down over in Arendal, and at once my mood is again as light as the sky above me. The grill is exactly where it ought to be, so too are, in a manner of speaking, your rock crystals, opals, amethysts, conches, and the silk blanket, even though it's news to me that our washroom has been turned into a treasure chamber.

Now let's go to sea.

IT IS, EVERY SINGLE TIME, a moment of truth.

I can think of no better expression to describe the experience of being at sea with you, in our boat. It is a moment of beauty, a moment that asks to be looked in the eye. It is perhaps the most demanding and rewarding moment I know of.

I sit at the back by the outboard motor. You sit in the front, always turned away from me, toward something else out there, as if you were scouting for land. I see your soles, which you rest on, your back, and I see your head, fair curls in the wind and the sharp light. You sit absolutely still. As long as the boat is moving you sit like this, motionless, your hands in your lap, facing something I don't know about. If we're headed for a wave so big that I have to shout "Wave!" you raise your hands from your lap almost like a sleepwalker and fold them around the rubber trim on each side, but you don't turn your head to see how we take the wave. When we've ridden it, you lay your hands back in place, in your lap. You don't seem interested. There is something thoughtless even about the way you give Balder a pat, when he puts his forepaws up on the thwart and presses his snout in between your hands. Usually I tell myself that you seem secure. It cannot be anxiety, I imagine, that is the source of so much serenity. But sometimes I catch myself thinking that perhaps you're hiding some unknown fear behind all this composure, and that's a thought that fills me with a nameless dread I don't know what to do with.

I've never asked you what you're thinking when you sit like that, turned away and averted. And you've never said anything. This mutual silence is a kind of agreement I am only reluctantly a party to, because at times it feels as though I'm losing you. You sit there, two or three short metres in front of me, but it's as though you've left me a long time ago, as though you're obeying orders from another and mightier captain, as though your ship has already brought you to a larger sea than I can reach with my little boat.

Where are you now, Gabriel?

I know your body so well, I see it clean through the jacket and trousers and vest, your skin and your muscle tissue, and I see that no quivers or tensions run through you. The blood flows effortlessly in your veins, your heart beats rhythmically and monotonously. You don't seem caught up in any agitation; no nagging want has set your glands pumping. Is it only that you're tuning in and tuning out? That the swell and the sea breeze soothe you? That you need this moment of leisure, that you're just resting and enjoying? You always say yes when I ask, but you're never the one who suggests a boat ride. Why not? I think. If it's something you need?

Are you okay, Gabriel?

You're so beautiful and dignified sitting there, somehow so very unattainable. Sometimes I can't stand it and I call your name out loud, above the headwind and the roar of the motor, to get you to look at me a moment. You turn, deliberately, as though you knew. I lay a kiss on the palm of my hand and blow it to you, mouth "I love you" with my lips and drink in your face with my eyes. You mime a sort of response, but your kiss lands in the water, for you don't have time to follow it all the way; you've already turned back to what is yours alone out there ahead.

Are you alone now?

No, you can't be. You are wholly and completely present in the landscape surrounding us, and I shrug off this melancholy that doesn't belong here where regret and longing have no place, here where there's so much space that even grief and joy become small and confused. I see how the open, exposed surroundings suit you, how you seamlessly fit yourself into the landscape, how it's yours. And I see how this context is also ours — father and son and dog on board a boat on its way out to sea. There's something timeless about this scene, something almost arche-typal, which makes it profoundly reconciliatory.

THE LINE OF SKERRIES outside our island isn't very long, but in compensation the good Lord has taken great pains with it. Even with only four weary horsepowers at our disposal we are within reach of bay, cliffs, islets, and points for every occasion, every prevailing wind, every angle of sunshine. But since the wind out here often blows from the north, and the sun is in the south during the daytime, we've developed the habit of choosing the smooth slopes of a little island some fifteen minutes away sailing southwest. At the back is a bluff that provides shelter from the wind, and in front it stretches out hungrily toward the open sea in the south.

That's where we're heading now. Apart from a couple of fishing boats there isn't a vessel in sight and therefore no people either. It's the way things usually are: as well as being paradisal — or perhaps precisely for that reason — the islands are blessedly free of people. At least those who haunt other coastlines with their noise, their engine power, and their incomprehensible haste.

On days like this the smooth rocky slopes are a dream, but they're no place to be when the wind suddenly turns and, for the sake of variety — or to spite the meteorologists — sends in storm troopers from the south. Then the waves bite their way onto the rocks in great mouthfuls and toss the boat ashore, and the wind whips away everything that isn't bolted down or held fast. Then the main force arrives, a black wall of sky that first appears low on the horizon and, before we've had time to ask each other if this can be true, it is towering above us in biblical dimensions and hurling down its heaviest ammunition.

Ha! I think, and picture to myself scenes of soaked discontent in charming Lillesand. For here the sun is beaming in the middle of October itself, and the sea splashes and smiles, and the wind is so apathetic it scarcely raises a flap.

THE BOAT IS MOORED, equipment and provisions carried ashore. Balder has caught the scent of something and is away over the hills. I busy myself with blankets and food, restore the little barbecue pit that wind, water, or vandals have ruined since our last visit. You stand there and watch in almost complete silence. I get undressed. The heat is Mediterranean and the body needs to store sunlight before the night of winter comes to claim us. I make myself comfortable on the blanket, light a cigarette and pour a glass of wine. I ask if you're hungry. I'll start the food shortly, just want to sit a little first and enjoy the sun. Do you want a glass of juice?

Each time I say, almost word for word, the same things. They're obvious things, but they have a liberating effect on you. You look around as though inspecting the site and you don't find anything that is incomplete or unusual, anything that isn't the way it usually is and therefore shouldn't be. You reply either "Yes please," or "No, I'll wait till later." And just that, simply the fact that you feel free and secure enough to choose your own answer, to follow your own inclination, to decide about your own thirst, tells me that you are ready. You are done with occupying the site, done with clearing it, accepting its restrictions and possibilities. Now you *are* here and could, if I were to suggest it, stay until next week.

How many times have we been here? A hundred? Two hundred? A thousand times? And yet each time you have to go through this laborious process of occupying and possessing the place. I can't help you in any way other than by doing everything the way we usually do it, in the same order, with the same things. Showing you that nothing has changed here. They say that the goldfish in its bowl has such a short memory that each time it swims round it's a new experience for it to reach the starting point once again. You, who have an associative memory that computer technology might envy, struggle with the opposite problem: until recognition has been established on an almost one-to-one basis you are hesitant and cautious, and dare not let yourself go.

Except at home, for inside the house other rules apply. There we have unwittingly — because we have a considerable talent for making a mess, if not always an equally great tolerance for it — trained you since you were small to live with shifting disorder. Let them say what they like, the therapists and the pedagogues, but I am in no doubt that the unpredictability at home has been good for you and has lifted a burden from your heavily laden shoulders — obviously because the framework, the walls of the house, and your family, has remained stable and unchanging. Had we made the effort, moreover, had we made it our full-time job to ensure that you would always find the cheese slicer in the same place, the tape in the third drawer under the glass cupboard, and the toothpaste to the right and not to the left of the bathroom tap, then I fear we would have made you anxious in your own home. Just the thought of your first having to inspect the house each time you returned from school, checking that everything was as it usually is, that the rug that yesterday lay horizontal on the floorboards in the living room did not today lie perpendicular or at a diagonal, that home was a place you were able to feel at home!

No, if we can't find the cheese slicer then we'll just have to teach you instead how to cut cheese with a knife. Because that's possible too, Gabriel. It's called improvising, which is exactly what I'm doing now, because believe it or not, I've managed to forget the brush to oil the chops with. How about that? We'll have to use our fingers instead. Want to help?

And, meticulously, you marinade the meat, first with your index finger, soon using your whole fist, delighted to have been almost ordered to mess with the food. As soon as the smells begin to waft from the grill, Balder runs up, tail wagging, and we chat away about this and that, nothing serious or important. The chops are juicy, the sun shines, and time flies. Not a word is mentioned about the lump of real gold you might be getting from Morten, for you are a prince and I am Your Highness, we're filthy rich, and full to bursting, but of course we've room for a bar of chocolate for dessert, and coffee and warm cocoa — we've room for anything, and soon we'll set out on a real treasure hunt again, because kings and princes can never get enough gold and silver and precious stones, that's precisely why they're kings and princes, and at home in our castle Queen Henni is waiting, and Princess Victoria, and there's Children's Hour on television, and we are something as simple and safe as a father and son and dog on our way home in a boat on a wonderful Tuesday evening in October.

CHAPTER FIVE

$\mathcal{T}$he gym is full. There are so many pupils here, and parents and brothers and sisters, that the teachers exchange small, conspiratorial winks and neglect to enforce the prohibition against climbing on the wall-bars when some of the bigger, more audacious children have a go. There has to be some elasticity to the rules: it's celebration time at school, and the air is already dense with tension.

Practice makes perfect, they say, and God knows there's been practising — at school, at friends' houses, at home. But it's one thing to stand in front of classmates, or in pairs in front of the bedroom mirror, or in the living room in front of Mom and Dad. To stand on stage, on the other hand, in front of all those many others, in front of unknown adults who live elsewhere, to be a debutant, even if it's in the gym — because tonight it doesn't look like a gym at all — is another story altogether. It's now or never, it's one single chance to succeed, to remember all the verses, all the steps, to look good in the dress, in the costume, the hairstyle — or to forget, stumble and stutter, and be a complete disgrace, to lose face and honour and never be able to look people in the eye again.

No, to be in second grade and perform at a school festival in front of a hundred, perhaps a hundred *and fifty* people, is no joke.

AT FIRST WE THOUGHT it had to be a joke, Mom and I. But your teacher was serious.

— This is something he's chosen himself and he can do it, she said firmly, with the sort of authority that only comes with a long life in teaching.

She's a wise and sensible woman, your teacher. She and the others who look after you at school, the Head Teacher, the Deputy Head, the Special Needs Teacher, and the Welfare Assistants. You are lucky — *we* are lucky. Every day we send you off to school, confident that you will be surrounded by people who wish you well, who stretch their patience and their budgets as far as they can in order to give you eventful, meaningful days. And if their patience runs out, as it does from time to time, they check themselves, take you outside and explain why, and you come home and explain to *u s* what happened and why, and perhaps you've learned something about how even the grown-ups at school can be impatient and make mistakes. And if their budgets run out, as they always do, then they improvise and dip into their own pockets rather than miss out on a two-day course in another town to learn more about the difficulties faced by this boy who's been placed in their care.

A "splendid," a "lovely" boy they tell us in your daily report, a "wonderful boy." Even though you sometimes bite them, hit, kick, throw stones, run off... when they don't get it right, no matter how hard they try. When you've had "not a good day," as they discreetly put it.

A couple of days before Christmas break you came home glowing with pride. You carried an enormous cup that looked remarkably like silver. This was after an autumn during which, in the course of a single week, you had acquired two skills that you'd persisted in persuading both yourself and the rest of us you would never learn to master: the art of reading and writing, and biking without training wheels. Your classmates had been doing both for a long time, and suddenly you became their equal. It happened so quickly that you could scarcely believe it, not until everyone in the schoolyard had seen you biking, and the whole class had heard you read. In recognition of these twin triumphs your teachers had chosen to buy a huge trophy, which now towers over the other treasures in your room.

I don't know which you were more proud of — your newly acquired skills or the trophy itself, the visible proof that you were valued as a winner by the adults at school. But I do know, Gabriel, that they all deserve a medal. Unfortunately, that won't happen, because the world isn't like that. People who do so much more, but say that they're only doing their job, don't mention it, it's a pleasure and we won't give up — people like that never get any medals. On the other hand, our gratitude is brightly polished and shining, and that they have. I know that they have yours too, which you express in your own way, with a hug and an unexpected smile, and with the greatest accolade of all: never once do you dread going to school.

— YES, BUT . . . ARE YOU really going to let Gabriel perform *on his own*, with a song?

— He'll be fine. We'll help him. Just make sure you practise regularly with him at home.

Again that weight of experience that makes a good teacher

hard to contradict.

And of course we'd practise, make our contribution to this … experiment. As long as it was something you yourself wished. When we asked if you wanted to do this, if you really wanted to stand alone on the stage and sing for all the others, you immediately replied yes. But a little too immediately, I thought. A little too overwhelmed, surprised to be asked at all, you who were usually excused from participating long before anyone thought of asking if you wanted to take part. Of course we would practise.

Learning the words and the melody came naturally to you. You have an auditory memory that at times can be eerie. Mom and I have experienced standing in the kitchen together, making dinner and conversing about things that concern only us, our voices kept low even though you're sitting in the far corner of the living room apparently minding your own business — and then a week, a fortnight later hear you repeat verbatim extracts from our conversation, usually introduced by: Why did you say to Mom that … ?

Or the two of us have returned from a shopping trip and you sit on the garden wall to finish your ice cream. As I stagger up the steps with the heavy plastic bags I hear a rendition in English, which is otherwise completely foreign to you, of the words and melody of a song from a CD I played for the first time in the car on the way home, while you sat and stared out of the window, seemingly totally disconnected.

To brush your teeth before you go to bed or to lock the car door as I must have told you to do a thousand times when we park outside the shopping mall are capsules of information that you seem to delete each time you're done using them. But a conversation not meant for your ears, the voice of a person you've scarcely met, the lyrics of a song, be it in Abkhazian — those you save at once. Yet I find no system to your criteria for deleting and saving, for what you pack away in oblivion and what you preserve in memory. Songs, verses, and lyrics that you've heard many times and that, if only for that reason, should be etched in your memory, you often forget between repetitions. The national anthem, for example, which you practise at school every year before National Day, or the psalm I have sung you to sleep with for years at your bedside.

Nor do I know whether you have a system or not. Probably your sorting principles are as enigmatic to you as they are to me. Besides, I suppose that you find the whole question strange and irrelevant — that is, after all, how you are.

NO, WORDS AND MELODY were soon mastered. You had, moreover, chosen that particular song because it was about something that interested you greatly.

I'm not sure whether it began with a video of *Captain Sabretooth* or with the cartoon film version of *Treasure Island*. In any case, it wasn't long before your greatest wish was to be a pirate yourself, albeit a good one, if such a thing were possible. For a long time you wished it so much that it was hard for you to accept that pirates belonged to "the old days" and didn't exist anymore, that you'd quite simply been born too late. Your engagement was so complete that there were times when we doubted whether or not you were aware of the difference between our house and your "castle," between our boat and your "ship," between seven-year-old Gabriel and "Captain" Gabriel. To some extent we played along, sometimes, I must confess, from motives that were less than pure — for example, to make you eat fish.

— Phooey! I'm no landlubber! Look, I can eat fish just like that!

Much more important than your attitude to fish, however, was your understanding of what was and was not real. We needed to know, to feel certain that you were quite clear about when something was "just pretend" and when it was "for real." Because you didn't play at buccaneering, you *went* buccaneering, and in that reality there were different rules. When, in keeping with these rules, you did something that was highly inappropriate and even dangerous according to the rules of ordinary reality, it was often difficult to reach you. If we addressed you with the logic and language of our world, you perceived it in your world as a kind of infringement of prevailing law and order, and the most awful scenes might ensue and last until you gave up, exhausted by tears and rage and despair. As we grew exhausted by our own despair, we gradually learned to take a different approach: to follow you into your world and, on its linguistic and logical terms, coax you back. If you sat digging in the dirt searching for an elusive treasure (which you at some "unconscious" level knew had to be there somewhere, you being the one who'd buried it!) and we needed you to come inside and change into clean clothes because dinner was waiting for us at Grandma's and Grandpa's, it would have led to several hours of disaster had we insisted and threatened with ordinary, exasperated parental authority. Far better to sacrifice a freshly ironed shirt, dig for the treasure together with you, and be just as aghast a pirate as you when Mom came out and told us she'd read in an old book that digging for gold ducats before nightfall could lead to eternal damnation. That was a language you understood:

— Then we've got to wait until it gets dark! Come on, let's go inside and wash off this *deadly* dangerous dirt!

— Yes, that's probably best, we answered, reckoning that a long Sunday dinner at Grandma's would fill your thoughts with other bounties.

It didn't always work, this strategy, and it demanded a lot of imagination and patience, but it did at least work often enough to make it worth the trouble. I'm not certain when it was that you gradually began to develop the ability to know, and to let us know that you were aware of what was "just pretend" and what was "for real." But two things certainly played their part: a play and a carnival.

AFTER A LOT OF HALF promises, late one summer we finally drove down to Kristiansand and the Zoo and Pirates' Bay. There you met them all, Pella and Pysa, Pinky and Ruben, Sunniva and Langemann, not to mention the glimpse you caught of Captain Sabretooth himself up at the top of a tower. We panned for gold and went into Gruesome Gabriel's treasure chamber, where you, very understandably, felt particularly at home. Then we went to sea on the pirate ship *The Black Lady* and spent a small fortune in the shops that sold pirate gear. It was fun and exciting, even for us adults, but at the same time it was a little disturbing: everything here was so consistent, so right and so "real" that it was hard for you to believe anything other than what you'd come to find confirmation of. Nor did it take long before you, with minimal indecision in your voice and eyes, proclaimed triumphantly:

— There, you see? There *are* real pirates! Only they live here on Kristiansand!

(For a long time you said that, "on," presumably in line with an unconscious logic that made pirates = treasure = island, so that the city of Kristiansand therefore had to be an island one was "on.")

The argument was, in a way, irrefutable. In the crowd around you pirates of the good old-fashioned type were actually strolling, sitting, and standing about — at least to the eyes of a child who was looking to see just that. Anyway, there was no reason to contradict you and spoil the day. Better to walk the plank, gather our last doubloons, and buy tickets for the evening's performance.

You were excited, naturally. You'd be allowed to stay up long past bedtime, and you'd finally get to see your alter ego, the King of the Seven Seas, Captain Sabretooth, at close range. You were even made up for the occasion — your face was painted skull-white — and you had a hat and moustache and were carrying a hook, a sword, and a pistol.

At first, when we entered the amphitheatre, you were a little uncertain. Even though we had repeatedly explained that this was a performance we were going to, a play, and you'd replied that of course you knew that, it evidently hadn't occurred to you that this implied, among other things, sitting down quietly in numbered rows and "just" being a spectator. All the same, it probably reassured you to see the other children looking just like you, with deathly pale faces and blood-red lips beneath stringy moustaches, and terrifying with all their weapons: they too had to find their places and sit down.

Then came the flames and the thunder and the music, so much light and sound that it took your breath away. It was impressive, overwhelming, and compelling, and once love and treachery, evil and heroism had all run their course, the good triumphed in the end, and everyone could join in and sing the closing song.

But you'd seen through something. You'd seen that the castle to the left was only a facade, that it wasn't real, that it was just scenery. You'd seen that the actors only appeared to kill and to be killed. You'd seen the floodlights and the microphones, the changes of scenery and the changes of costume, and you'd understood that this was just theatre, this was just pretend. Not even Captain Sabretooth was for real — he was standing there on the stage smiling and bowing and inviting the audience to come back some other time. Maybe even his treasure wasn't for real?

You didn't say these things then, nor have you spoken of them since. But I could see that you were more than suspicious, that you pondered the possibility that Mom and Dad might have a point, that perhaps real pirates didn't exist anymore.

Your suspicion was strengthened a few months later when we invited your class to the house for a pirates' carnival. We'd worked hard on invitations made like treasure maps, with singed edges and drops of candle wax, and they all came, armed to the teeth and in their finest costumes. Even Mom and I were dressed up in homemade pirate finery. It was a marvellous evening, you all went treasure hunting around the house, and you got sweets and money and gold — of chocolate, admittedly — but everyone was happy, including you. All the same, it was as if you now knew and no longer just suspected: pirates are something you play at, not something you can be for real.

Since then there's been a half-heartedness about your sessions of playing at pirates. It's as if it doesn't seem worth the effort anymore. And it hasn't been as difficult for us to coax you out of your pirate role — if not of all the other roles. A lost innocence, perhaps, but above all a triumph for maturity, a big step on the road to gaining an understanding of who you are in the world.

And we'll just have to put up with the fact that you're no longer afraid of being called a landlubber. There are more important things in life than eating fish.

— ARE YOU SURE you want to do this, Gabriel? You can do exactly what you want, no one at school will say anything if you change your mind. You know that, don't you?

— Yes, I know that. But can't I do it if I want to? Please,

please, please? I know it, here, just listen…

And you launch into your song, both verses. You do it impeccably, strictly speaking, even though you also demonstrate beyond any doubt that you're your parents' true-born son and that you, like them, would be wise to choose a career other than music.

But this wasn't about music. This was about longing and your need to be seen the way you saw that others were seen. It was about being included by the others, something you hardly ever experience ordinarily, at least not outside school hours. That treat is so exceptional for you that on the rare occasions when children your own age call on you at home you're completely perplexed. You lose your conceptions, as you put it, without being quite sure what that means. Do you remember that day last summer when Marit from your class suddenly rang the doorbell? First she gave you a hug that left you embarrassed and almost lost for words, and then she asked if you wanted to go out and play. You were so busy expressing your amazement that you almost forgot to answer her:

— Can you imagine, Dad? Someone in my class wants to visit me! And in the middle of summer holidays too!

Yes, of course you wanted to be part of it, of course you wanted to sing, and of course you wanted to do it on a stage in front of the class and all the others. Of course you wanted to show them that you too could do it, that you were one of them.

YOU ASK MANY and difficult questions, Gabriel, but some of them are difficult in complicated ways. If others had asked them, I might have perhaps considered them rhetorical and a bit stupid. When you're the one asking, however, I see and hear that they are deeply serious questions, born of a pain in you that won't go away, no matter how often you ask them, for they have no answers. They are questions like:

— Why can't I be like the others?

— Because, son, because ... you're different.

It isn't a good answer and I know that. All the others are different too, and yet you're unlike them. And it hurts you — more because you don't understand why you're different than because you actually are. The latter you can, in a sense, come to terms with. The former is a riddle with no answer, and you're condemned to live with it.

But even if you're different, you're not alone, Gabriel. Spread around the world are millions of people who struggle with the same sorts of problems as you do, even though they do so in other ways and with different preconditions. What unites you is that you don't understand, you don't master the social games that go on around you and seem so utterly easy and natural to the rest of us.

Still you're right, in a way, when you protest almost accusingly against such attempts to calm you and comfort you, when you express doubt that anyone else *in the whole world* can have the same problems as you, because no two people are exactly similar, so no two people can have exactly similar problems. You say this with a certainty I don't quite know how to interpret. Is it simply a logical inference you're formulating? Are you talking about a painful and perhaps unconscious insight that stems from your experience of being different? Or is it that you find strength and security in the experience of being the only one? Sometimes it seems as though you derive comfort from this very undefinability, as when you came home one day shortly after the start of a new school year and exclaimed happily, as though it were a great encouragement:

— Hey, Mom, it's so great — we've got a girl in our class who's different! Yeah, not different like me, but different from the others!

Your classmates are exceptional. From the very first day at school they've embraced you with a natural compassion that is free of any strained sympathy or adult-induced sense of obligation. They can tease you and shout at you, they can quarrel with you and have mock fights with you, they can also have real fights with you if they or you make it necessary; but they have a kind of built-in understanding of where your limits are, of what you're able to accept and tolerate, of what happens when you suddenly turn very Gabriel, and of what they then ought to do and definitely not do. Perhaps part of the explanation is that from the very beginning we've tried to be open with both them and their parents by giving, among other things, explanatory talks about you at parents' meetings and class gatherings. But most of all it's just blessed good luck: you've been lucky enough to end up among children who probably don't always understand you and perhaps don't even always like you, but who nevertheless, or perhaps for that very reason, wish you well.

I never saw this more clearly than on National Day. Like most of the other festive holidays children look forward to, May 17 isn't a good day for you. The expectations are so immense and diffuse that they can't possibly be met, the level of noise so high, the crowd so great, the impressions so manifold. You lose track of things, and the ability to concentrate, you become confused and that makes you dispirited. And yet each year we try, because we'd so much like for you to feel included.

This time you have, uneventfully, but also with no apparent pleasure or understanding of the point of it, marched in the morning procession and carried the flag from school to church. Afterwards we've been to town and bought a cap gun, ice cream, and a sausage roll. Now we're going to school, where there will be speeches and games and competitions. You and your schoolmates have shot your way through most of your ammunition, and because everybody else is, you too want to take part in the race on the sports field. The event is organized by classes, and prospects of huge gold medals are held out to the winners. One of those, you say, you've just *got* to have, and you decide, as though it were a matter of pure will, to win.

I stand behind you on the starting line, and with a lump in my stomach, explain that you mustn't begin to run before you hear "Ready, Steady" — and then the starting gun. Great doses of adrenalin and excitement are pumping through you, but you confirm that you've understood.

— Ready... Steady...

The crack comes so suddenly and unexpectedly that you need a moment to compose yourself. But you feel the thrust of my hand on your back, hear the cheering from the sidelines, and see that the others are off. You stride out, you run like you've never run before, narrow-eyed and determined. You run to win, to get that medal, to show them, and then ... you look around and see that you're all alone, that there's just you and the gravel field, that way ahead the others are already crossing the finishing line, and you realize that you've lost.

A terrible NO! explodes from your throat, and you collapse into a fetal position in the middle of that sea of gravel and weep convulsively. A moment later I'm there, sitting with you and holding you tight against my chest, not knowing what to say or do. An awkward silence descends upon the field; people look over at one another and out at us.

Then they're there, your classmates, all of them, swarming

round you. I can hardly believe what I'm hearing.

— You were great, Gabriel!

— You did it, Gabriel!

— What a good runner you are, Gabriel!

You raise tearful, disbelieving eyes to look at them, and the trace of a crooked smile appears on your face.

— Come on, Gabriel, let's go and get your medal!

— Yes but, I didn't win…

— Of course you won, Gabriel!

— You were brilliant, Gabriel!

— Come on, come and fetch your medal, Gabriel!

You stand up and dry your face on your sleeve, and radiate pure, unadulterated pride and joy as your classmates lead you to the trophy table. Out on the gravel field I remain sitting with my own tears, moved as rarely before by what these seven- and eight-year-old children have done for you, just because they wished you well.

IT'S BEEN A FORTNIGHT since May 17. Fourteen May days are a long time in a child's mind, long enough time to leave things behind and get on, but today is the school's cultural evening, and I haven't forgotten that scene on the gravel track. The lump in my stomach is back, only bigger.

As usual, when it's something important, I've left the camera at home. Your classmates' parents and the parents of other children you know come over and wish us luck. They probably haven't forgotten either. Some of them offer to take photos when it's your turn.

The program is extensive this evening. Individually or in small groups, thirty second-graders are going to sing, dance, recite, or perform sketches. I must admit I remember very little of what happened. I see that some of the bigger pupils are dangling from the wall-bars with the tacit permission of the teachers, and I picture you standing and waiting in the locker room where we left you, a somewhat distant look in your eyes, but more because you sense an unusual level of tension among your fellow pupils than because you're tense yourself. Out in the gym hall, Mom and I are feeling a little uncomfortable, almost stared at. We try to talk about other things while we wait, but as always when the conversation absolutely has to be about something else, it comes back around to you. In the end we sit there in silence. Victoria finds acquaintances with whom to while away the waiting time.

The lights go down and the teacher takes the floor to welcome us and say a few well-chosen words about what she's proud to present to us this evening. Then the annual cultural evening for the district school's second grade is underway.

I can't follow what's going on, I'm much too nervous. I'm in

Nicaragua. There's a big surprise waiting for you there, which I haven't told you about. During a visit a few months earlier, in connection with an aid project, I met somebody who introduced me to someone else who knew the boss of a breeding station outside Managua. I paid a hefty price, but things like this don't come cheap, and then the fees, to the vet, to the agricultural department, to the export authorities, plus a few other governmental bodies. The diplomats at the Norwegian embassy and good contacts among people in high office did their best, but there wasn't enough time. It turned out that the Norwegian authorities required six months notice to okay the import, and I had to return home empty-handed. But all the same — in an accredited and well-run breeding station in Nicaragua — it's waiting for you. It's yours, Gabriel, only it lives somewhere else. Green as spring grass, speckled with all the colours of the rainbow, the most loquacious breed, found only in the depths of America, which for you doesn't mean the U.S., but Latin and South America, because what are fast cars and skyscrapers compared to the mysteries and wonders of the jungle, incarnate in the eloquent bird that sits perched on the shoulder of every self-respecting pirate, a genuine...

— ...which he has chosen himself and which he will now sing for us. Please, Gabriel.

Never before has a gym been this quiet. You walk out onto the floor, position yourself in front of the microphone, cast a glance at the guitarist who's to accompany you, and look out across the hall. You appear neither afraid nor uncertain, more as though you're trying to get an overall picture of the unusual situation, as of a complicated traffic picture. Around you, on the other hand, the tension is palpable. Two hundred, perhaps three hundred eyes see only you. Silent prayers fill the air.

Ready... Steady...

The first chord sounds like a starting gun, but this time you're prepared. You empty your eyes — and you sing. You sing! You don't stumble, you don't stutter, you don't forget a single line, not so much as a word. You sing systematically and confidently and flawlessly

> *I am a parrot from the jungle deep*
> *Where I was born a long time ago.*
> *My parrot mama said, because I couldn't speak:*
> *Give him time, he'll talk, I know*

and you don't see it, but there are tears in two hundred eyes, tears of joy, tears of relief, proud tears, and when you've finished both your verses and the final chords die away and you bow deeply, the ovation is thunderous.

We stand up, the whole room stands up, we clap and cheer and shout bravo and dry our tears, and you smile crookedly and happily and take another bow. You've done it; you've shown them that you can too, that you're one of them.

But I look at all these people who now stand applauding, hailing you for what you've just achieved on stage. They are the same people who, fourteen days ago, stood and watched you fall to pieces on the gravel field, and we all know that what you've done now is much more than show us you can sing in front of an audience. Because that day on the sports field you laid bare, you screamed out a nakedness that only a very few would confess to. And what's more, tonight you have, on behalf of us all, surmounted it.

CHAPTER SIX

*D*o you remember the day of the fire?

I didn't wake suddenly, because sleep was strong and held on tightly to the prey it had been hunting for most of the night. But the noise was stronger, an insistent knocking that didn't belong here where only crying seagulls and bleating sheep have an established right to disturb the early-morning peace. Slowly and laboriously, as though constantly having to stop to decompress, consciousness rose to the surface. As it finally broke through I heard clearly: someone was shouting and hammering on a door.

My first thought was you. What were you doing out, what

had happened? A queue of possible and impossible answers at once formed, and then dissolved just as quickly, for in the bed beside me you too were waking up. I had slept in the guest room so that I could get up with you without waking Mom, and you must have come down to me at some point in the night.

The sound of shouting and hammering did not stop. It only grew louder the clearer my head became.

— Carry on sleeping, I'll be right back, I said.

I grabbed a pair of trousers and a shirt, threw them on, and staggered out the door and up the stairs. On the way into the living room I saw Mom coming out of the bedroom in her dressing gown, a sleepy question in her eyes. The Easter sun had already risen, and in the sharp backlight through the window we saw the outline of a woman. She stood there pounding with her fist on the terrace door. In the crook of one arm she was holding a small dog.

I didn't recognize her immediately, but Mom saw that it was the tenant of a neighbouring house a couple hundred metres behind us. When we opened up, we were met by a dissolved and tear-streaked face and a garbled, almost hyperventilated flood of words. We tried to get her to come in, but she wouldn't, stood still with the dog squeezed under her arm and repeated the same shouted words over and over again. We recognized one of them: fire. At the same moment we realized that what we had taken for morning mist in the east was actually clouds of smoke coming from the house behind the barn.

We knew that she lived alone there with her little daughter, and were suddenly gripped by an anxious fear. I grabbed her firmly by the shoulders and shook her and tried to fix her gaze: Is your daughter in the house? In reply she only wept and cried out fragmented sentences that were impossible to make any sense of. We repeated the question several times, and I felt a touch of panic as we picked up phrases like "inside the house" and "must get out." We managed to get her into the living room and down into a chair, and Mom set off running. I was to ring the emergency services and try to calm the woman down, attempt to get a definite answer out of her and find the fire-fighting equipment.

It's incredible how quickly it is possible to think. While on the phone and at the same time trying to pacify the woman, I saw Mom through the window, running, and it was as if I were running with her, racing to get there first. Even in the midst of two desperately important conversations I had all the time in the world to think: What does one do with a burned child, a child who has inhaled smoke? Can the doctors do anything at all for her? It looks like a fine day; we should go out in the boat. There's a bit of a breeze blowing from the southeast, I can see that from the smoke, so the little island isn't a good idea today. Is it true that our neighbour's house is a burning house? How shall I tell the mother that she has lost her daughter?

WE NEARLY LOST YOU ONCE, we thought. You were just six, seven, maybe eight weeks old, I don't remember. It was late in the evening and time for your feeding. You, who had always been so ravenous, who could never get enough, lay weak and feeble in the bed without even the strength to take the breast into your mouth. You disappeared from us, were on the point of leaving, and your body was burning. We shook you in terror, tried to call you back, turned and lifted your head. Mom forced breast and milk in between your lips, and late in the night you finally opened your eyes. You had a frighteningly high fever, but it passed, and you came back to us.

We almost lost Alexander even before he was born, in a nasty car accident; someone ran into Mom and permanently damaged her knee. Incredibly, the fetus that was due to be born in three weeks time was unhurt. Since then we've nearly lost him on several other occasions, to forces and urges that tried to appropriate both his love of life and his life itself. But we got him back too.

Sometimes we have also lost each other, lost sight of each other in the turmoil, in the fog of everyday life, in the mist of habit, in new and unfamiliar faces. But we found the way back and returned home.

We can't afford to lose more than the time that passes by itself, Gabriel. What we have left is too little.

HOW FIRES WREAK HAVOC with the discretion of closed doors! Like family quarrels, personal tragedies, abuse. When Mom opened the front door and entered the vestibule, all she sensed was the smell and the heat. Then she pushed open the door to the hallway, and I picture the flames hissing to her, telling her that she would lose herself in there.

She was standing on the stoop, choking as she gasped for breath, as I came running with the fire extinguisher and news that the daughter was probably safe: there was another little dog still in there — I thought. The mother's speech was still incoherent, so I could not be sure; perhaps a little girl really was dying inside the house. I wrapped my shirt around my nose and mouth and dived into the blackness, but was at once blinded and struggling for breath. A living black wall of sooty smoke engulfed the air around me, sucked it out of my lungs and left something there instead that my body refused to absorb. I did not want to, but I had to get out, and then it was my turn to kneel on the stoop. Afterwards we emptied the extinguisher through a window, to precious little avail. The house was consumed by fire, and our attempts to put it out merely a joke. Besides, we could now hear the sound of sirens from over the hill and it was time to make way for the experts.

It was only then that I realized you were standing there watching, barefoot and in pajamas, and with our garden hose in your hand. You had pulled it loose from the tap and dragged it with you in order to help, with no definite plan of how to fill it with water, but all the more with a desire to be of assistance. I went over to you and wrapped my arms tightly around you, as though you had just been rescued from the sea of flames. I could not rid myself of the image of a little girl in there. We still did not know whether this was a hideous death by fire, or only a sad story about a house that burned down, and perhaps a dog that died.

WE LOSE SO MANY THINGS, Gabriel. We lose all the time, and we grieve for what is gone. Or perhaps we grieve most for the feeling of loss, the certainty of having lost, rather than for what we have lost. Ask me, because I know grief.

Do you want to know about grief? Shall I explain grief to you?

It still happens, though not as often as before, in the beginning, the first years, that grief strikes. Now it happens at intervals of weeks and months, but it always happens suddenly and unexpectedly, as in an ambush, and each time it overwhelms me, overrides everything else and makes me turn away and cry a little.

I don't know if I can explain grief to you, Gabriel, even though perhaps you already know it, but under other names, that hurt in other ways. My grief is adult and difficult. It isn't your confusion when you don't understand, when your thoughts crash, as you put it, and you can't manage to think any of them all the way through. Nor is it the despair you might experience then, that makes you scream and weep and hit out in anger, that makes you look at me with wounded, pleading eyes, praying that I explain to you why, why, why. The despair you lie down with on the floor, pressed up against a wall or a piece of furniture, powerless and ashamed. Nor is grief the embarrassment you struggle with afterwards, once it's over, when you compel your gaze to defy shyness, to bring it back from the remote emptiness in which it has sought refuge and, with defenceless-ness in your eyes ask if I love you anyway, if we can be friends again forever.

What can I tell you about grief?

Grief is as big as the sky and the universe, as big as infinity, which we've talked about and none of us understands. Grief is as big as the riddle you puzzle all of science with, just by being you. As big as inscrutability, as big as the tiny little seed life neg-lected to plant in you, your difference, the absence that will always follow you and fill me with grief.

But this isn't an answer, I know that. Forgive me.

There's a grief in everything, Gabriel, in the flowers and the rain, in treasures and dreams. Grief is losing, grief is not to have. Grief is certainty. Grief is life that slips, time that passes, what could have been, but was not. Grief is helpless-ness. There's room for everything in the mansion of grief. It's dark and snug in the mansion of grief, and it's lonely. Grief is to catch the wind, grasp water in your fist. Grief is quiet. Grief is polite. It comes, and then it goes away. But grief is never gone. Only things are gone when they disappear. Grief is impossible, Gabriel.

THE FIREMEN ARRIVED, and the police, and it was eventu-ally established that the daughter was safe — she had spent the night at her grandparents. The other little dog, which had been stuck inside the house when the mother came over to us, had probably run out when Mom or I opened the door and tried to get in. It was found in good shape.

Neither of these two happy endings affected you. All that interested you were the uniforms, the equipment, the jets of water and the very big and very red fire engines.

More locals and a lot of children had turned up, and now that the fire no longer threatened tragedy and death, it became an occasion. Some popped back home to fetch a Thermos, others their cameras, and we stood around in groups and talked about the possible causes, and the living-room window that looked as if it might explode at any moment under the pressure, and what a shame it was about the house, newly redecorated and all, and what a gorgeous day it looked to become. Even the firemen and the policemen strolled over for a chat during their breaks, and all things considered it was a fine morning hour — all the more so since the owners of the house were off in the mountains, so no one felt under any obligation to temper their good mood with tactful, head-shaking empathy.

By late morning everyone had had enough, the firemen, the spectators, and the local paper. It was over. A soot-stained and boarded-up shell surrounded the burned-out core of the house — it was said that the flames had eaten a full inch into the tim-bered walls. Only the insurance company could seek to profit from what was left. We went home, packed food and drink, and took off to sea.

YOU SPOKE LITTLE TO US that day, wandered around a great deal on your own. Mom and I bathed in the sun, happy and carefree. Perhaps it was because the day had already been so eventful, perhaps because we have taught ourselves to grab whatever free time offers itself, perhaps simply because we were thoughtless — but we didn't speak much to you either.

What did you think? All the fuss, the fire engines, this

whole unusual day must have made an impression on you. But what? How?

You have, in your own particular way, a strong ability to feel with others. Not conventionally, in the expected manner, but strongly all the same. Sometimes your empathy can seem heedless because it is tactless. And you do not forget, you feel for a long time. About a year and a half after one of the special needs teachers at school had lost her husband you went up to her one day and said:

— Hey, Karin?

— Yes, Gabriel?

— It's been such as long time now since your husband died that I think it's time for us to find you a new one.

You meant well; Karin who knows you understood that. But you don't understand, have no possibility of understanding that when one means well one can also do damage, as when you pick an itching scab off a wound that should be allowed to heal undisturbed. For people who don't know you it isn't easy to deal with a little boy who approaches in the street and asks, with genuine concern in his eyes:

— You're so fat, why don't you eat less?

You feel sorry for others and would like to help and comfort them — this is something you often express. You mean what you say and I don't doubt that. But I am not sure why you mean it. Is it because you've learned that what one should do to be kind and nice is to help and show consideration, to be generous and comforting? Or does it come from an unselfish impulse in you, an altruistic need to offer support? I don't know, and I probably never will know, and perhaps the questions are academic, irrelevant to the practicalities of our everyday life.

One day when we had been discussing your problems you fell silent for a moment before saying:

— Well at least I know what *your* problem is!

— Oh yes? And what's that?

— You can't eat apples and pears and nuts and stuff. That's *your* problem.

It was, as far as it went, true. I do have an allergy, but it was a pretty unusual comparison to draw.

Half an hour later at the dinner table you returned to the subject:

— Hey, Dad, if I save until my piggy bank is full, d'you think I'll be able to afford to buy some pills for you so that you can eat apples and pears and nuts and stuff? If there are such pills, that is?

You'd forgotten the original purpose of your savings — to buy the biggest diamond in the world.

BUT DO YOU KNOW WHAT regret is? Oh yes, when things disappear and you lose them, or when you break them and lose them in that way, you can feel regret. But your regret is always turned against circumstances, never something you yourself have done, and could have left undone. You have never broken a cup in a regrettable moment of inattention, nor ever taken your eye off a lost copper coin. The cup was wet and it slipped, or somebody slammed a door and gave you a start. The coin was so little and the house so big, and you had other things to do than to look for it, and it's easy for the adults to say, but children aren't good at remembering where they put things. In this way you channel your regret outside yourself and direct it at a world that never takes enough responsibility and is always open to blame.

— It's *your* fault, you say to time and the wind, and don't ask for a reply, don't need a reply.

The only exception is in relation to your problems, which you don't understand and therefore fear might be your own responsibility — at least if I'm to go by the seriousness in your voice on those occasions when you ask if they are your fault. All I can do then is repeat, Gabriel, that you're completely innocent. Your problems are no more your own fault than are your fair curls or your strong muscles. You are born with them, created that way by nature.

It often doesn't take more than that to placate you. As long as someone other than yourself is to blame — be it nature herself — then you can quietly put your worries behind you and carry on. You have weighed an opportunity to feel regret and guilt, and found it wanting.

I envy you this ability. Personally, I regret far too much.

On the other hand you largely lack the ability to generalize, to transfer experience and learning from one situation to another. Or more accurately: it is difficult for you to adapt to new situations the way the rest of us do, by using experiences from similar, but not identical, situations. Whereas life for us might be described as a succession of consecutive but discrete events, each one calling for a uniquely crafted response and a carefully adapted type of behaviour, you tend to approach most situations with a kind of standard behaviour. Your instinctive understanding of situations is underdeveloped, and you therefore make use of a narrow range of fairly crude patterns of response. It is as though you decide at once, when confronted by a situation, whether it calls for irritation, for example, or anticipation, joy, anger, or sympathy. And once the decision is made, you respond with an appropriate, standardized behaviour. If you find reason to feel annoyed, you will feel it as much, and in the same way, whether the provocation is small and unimportant, or large and serious. If it seems to you that sympathy is called for, then you are as effusive, whether it be to comfort a member of the family or a stranger in the street who seems unhappy to you.

To put it in another way, you lack a sense of proportion. You don't dose the intensity of your behaviour and your feelings to accord with the individual situation, no more than you, for example, pitch the level of your voice to take into account how far away the person you're talking to happens to be. Sitting just half a metre away from me at the dinner table, you might address me with a volume that would be more appropriate if I were at the far end of the house. It is not because you lack the ability to distinguish between loud and quiet speech, but — as is so often the case — because you almost exclusively use your own criteria as the basis for your behaviour. Since you do not understand, or are unable to empathize with other people's unspoken premises, motivations, and desires in a given situation, you ignore them and act as though your own premises, motivations, and desires are the only valid ones. So you raise your voice — not because it is necessary for me to hear you, but because you believe you have something important to say and that other voices therefore must either give way to yours or be drowned out, regardless of whether what they might have to say might also be important. Only if I expressly state that now you must listen, now *I* have something important to tell *you*, do you fall silent and listen. But on your own you are unable to "read" the situation, and gather from the expression on my face, the impatience in my voice and the raised eyebrows, or from all the countless hints that populate a social situation, that now it is someone else's turn to speak.

Of all the many problems you have to face, my son, this is perhaps your greatest handicap. For even if in some given circumstance I explain to you that here you must show consideration for others, that social insight has disappeared by the time the next situation arises. That which you learned a moment ago has no transferable validity for a succeeding situation. Only if an identical situation arises are you able to use what you have learned. In a sense, you are a kind of social fundamentalist: each social occasion has, for you, its own absolute value and exclusive status, which make experiences gleaned from it unusable in the next. Whereas life for the rest of us is a steady stream of occasions that interlock with one another and allow us to accumulate appropriate patterns of behaviour, it seems to me that for you it consists rather of a series of discrete situations that must be approached individually, one after the other, and each time as though for the first time. I can only imagine how tiring and frustrating it must be, and how tempting it must seem to you to be spared the involvement and the empathizing with what others think and feel.

Like that time when a scene at home ended with Mom smashing a pan of mashed potatoes down on the oven so hard that the whole ceramic surface cracked. After observing the performance in silence you made your only comment:

— Next time you buy powdered mash, Dad, buy two packets in case Mom gets angry.

BY LATE AFTERNOON, sated with sun and grilled food, we were ready to head for home. Mom had climbed up a rise to have a look around and see where you were, and called me to join her. Somewhere behind our house a thick grey bank of fog swayed, in complete isolation. It couldn't be possible.

But it was. When we got home we saw that the fire engines and the police were back, and the spectators in their places. A small, overlooked cinder somewhere up under the roof, and the draft from a broken window, had been enough. Seeming this time playful and teasing, the flames licked again across the walls as embarrassed firemen hosed and chopped away at the charred timbers.

WE LOSE WHAT WE MUST LOSE, Gabriel — because time is finished with it, because time is up, because nothing lasts after it is over. Not houses, not friends nor people, not even old trees last any longer than they should, than their allotted span of time. Sometimes I miss you already. I miss your time, the one that is gone and lives on in memory, and the one to come, the one that is anticipation, the one you shall fill with your own losses when you yourself have lost and have been lost.

We are only unlosable to ourselves, my son. Everything else loses us.

CHAPTER SEVEN

I sit here and look at my hand, Gabriel, at all that is written down there. Most of it is illegible. It is scribbled in haste, in languages I don't understand, a line here, a scar there, a mark and a hollow. Some people would have us believe that hands are ready-written books we are born with, two volumes in which our lives are chronicled in creases and wrinkles even before we have lived, reference books that we can consult to learn who we are and that can tell us what will become of us. But it isn't so. Our hand-books are written by ourselves, or life writes them for us day by day, so that nothing shall be forgotten, so that each blow and each caress shall be retained and remembered. Just as the sole of your foot carries on it the impress of every grain of sand and soft carpet it has walked on, every door it has kicked in, so is carved into your hands the stem of every flower, every coin, and every bar you have grasped.

That is why it's so good to hold someone else by the hand, for then two stories talk to each other. Like when we're driving the car, me in front and you in the back, and one of us suddenly just has to hold out his hand and take the other's for a moment, and a transmission takes place of something we never speak of, but which is good and great and strong. In the library of the body only the eyes process more information on our lived lives than the hands, but they cannot be read, as the hands can. If God exists when we die, I imagine that it is our hands he will ask to see. Then he will smile or grieve, for the hand-writing cannot be rubbed out, it is the journal we keep throughout our life, and we shall be judged upon it.

I sit here and look at my hand, and it is like a treasure map. Had I been able to decipher all the signs and read them in the right order, I might have uncovered my whole history. But that I cannot do, that would be like living life over again. We never quite manage to find ourselves, Gabriel; it is a futile and fruitless search.

We can, however, be found, and we can ourselves find others. *That* is the real miracle of the hands — that they let us receive and that they let us give. All the rest is finally just reading matter to pass the time.

Now I offer you my hand in support. With the other I hold on to the rusting chain that stops the boat from drifting so far away from land that it would make your clambering jump up onto the pier too long and too difficult. And then it's your turn to hold, hold on tightly to the rope as I lift the chest from the bottom of the boat, from the depths of this unreasonably low tide, raise it up above my head like a sacrificial offering and shove it carefully onto the edge of the pier. Finally I follow up with the rest of the equipment.

We're on Treasure Island. It has another name, but we don't use that now. Places have many names; they're called houses, fortresses, castles, or palaces, all according to time and usage. Today this place is called Treasure Island, for today we're off on a treasure hunt, so it can't have the same name as when we're only going for a walk, or to visit Jon Ivar in the lighthouse. Names are important. Without them we don't know where we are or what we're doing there. Without names we wouldn't even have treasures to talk about, only rocks and metal. Names make things genuine and valuable, and false treasures are worthless, they're not worth collecting. No one knows that better than you.

Gradually we have developed a certain routine. We know what we're searching for, and where it's most likely to be found. Before, you remember, when we were beginners, we dug our spades into any old patch of ground, chipped away at random rock faces, and dived down aimlessly to arbitrary seabeds. It wasn't always easy to hide the disappointment when we did not immediately come across buried chests, when diamonds and nuggets of gold did not fall away of their own accord from the rock, when schooners laden with precious loot didn't appear to us among the forest of kelp. You thought it was unjust and unfair, and that we had better move to Africa or America, since it was obvious others had been here before us and found whatever was to be found. When I objected that this might possibly present difficulties, you thought me stupid and frivolous, and that I didn't understand much about what was really important.

After numerous unsuccessful expeditions we gradually came to an agreement that the important thing was to *find*. How what we found happened to be located just where we had chosen to look was a matter of secondary importance and something we could safely disregard. It was none of our concern whether it had been left behind by pirates of old, or overlooked by earlier gold diggers, or even put there so that it could be found later. All that mattered was our finding it.

And we certainly did begin to find, one gem after the other. Opals and lapis lazuli, which are normally found only in Bolivia or Afghanistan, miraculously cropped up in a corner of the garden, and crystals and copper coins glinted in the sunlight between the rocks on the shore. Now we were able to make reliable treasure maps, certain in our knowledge that beneath the sign of the crossed bones at the end of the track, there would lie an amethyst or two.

On your own account you experimented with a variation that didn't prove quite as successful, because it isn't always easy to tell the difference between a smart game and being simply outsmarted. You realized that after you had been out on one of your expeditions and found the skeleton of a sheep's head. You pulled out the teeth, placed them in a glass of water on the bedside table, and then were mightily irritated to discover next morning that nothing had happened. The teeth had not turned into money. Not until you were given a thorough explanation of the fact that the tooth fairy probably can't be fooled, and is well able to tell the difference between human teeth and sheep's teeth, did you accept the fact that this was not a shortcut to riches.

TODAY WE'RE NOT SURE what we might find. Perhaps we won't find anything at all, perhaps rascals and bandits have been here before us and run off with everything of value. We mention this possibility to each other, this outrage that in no way seems unthinkable to us. We dwell on it in silent unease as we make our way across the uneven island terrain, carrying your heavy treasure chest between us. It would be almost too good to be true if other treasure hunters hadn't discovered the grotto we're on our way to explore, which previous visits have shown to contain so many wondrous things. But we don't talk out loud about such things, because you never know — hidden behind every rock may be a wrongdoer with cutlass and musket at the ready, eavesdropping and spying on us. We don't breathe a word about our real destination, but drop loud and misleading hints about a notorious treasure-free cave on the other side of the island as we glance about on all sides in search of telltale signs of fiendish charlatans and unspeakable buccaneers.

On the slope below the lighthouse we decide to take a break — not only because waffles and cocoa would taste good, but also because our pursuers then will think we're just taking an ordinary walk, and go back home in frustrated resignation. The treasure, which has already been awaiting us since time immemorial, can wait a few more minutes. But not too many! Though you have never admitted to having butterflies in your stomach — the thought repels you, those poor butterflies — it's easy to see that your whole body is tingling with excitement and anticipation. Before I'm halfway through my drink, you just *have* to go on ahead.

I remain behind, sitting on a rock. I light a cigarette, and before I've smoked it you're back gasping for breath, disturbed, your gaze flickering about. It was too dark, it was too scary, you don't dare on your own. Because it might be that not *all* the villains have gone home, perhaps some are still waiting in there where you can't see them, hatching the most sinister and wicked plans to trick you into telling them where the treasure is.

AT PLAY YOU ARE a master in conjuring forth fear, you who in everyday life know no fear. Even the police have experienced this. One day, when Mom's car broke down on the way home from work, and she knew that the taxi was due to drop you off at home any minute, she was driven there at top speed by a friendly patrol-car officer. But it was too late; you had already come home from school and found the house empty. When you then heard Balder begin to bark at the sound of an unknown car approaching, you resolutely made your way down into the library and pulled a heavy Mexican machete out of its sheath, even though you weren't allowed to: this was an emergency, the house had to be protected, and you had to protect yourself against unknown intruders. The policeman who was with Mom was met in the doorway by a fearless youngster with a jungle sword raised high over his head, ready to strike, and had to back away in alarm ... An imaginary peril, on the other hand, of an encounter with wily villains in a treasure grotto, you daren't face that without someone to cover your back.

To be afraid is not to know. Sometimes I think the only thing you really fear is yourself, about whom you know the least. Is that why you sometimes ask, cautiously as always when you want to talk about your problems:

— Are they dangerous?

No, Gabriel. Your problems are not dangerous, at least not in the same way as, for example, cancer or a heart attack, illnesses you can die of. Nor are they dangerous in the sense that they can cause you physical pain, like a wound. And they are definitely not dangerous to others — you cannot "infect" other people.

The only time your problems can be dangerous is when no proper account is taken of them. A person who feels himself systematically misunderstood, ignored, and ridiculed, and who doesn't understand why, nor is given any help to understand why, can with time develop a strong strain of aggression that affects other people. On the other hand, there is nothing at all to suggest that you have a greater likelihood than others of turning to violence. Rather the opposite: when you're driven into a rage, into shouting and punching and screaming, I can see by the tears you don't even try to hide that it is as much yourself you are punishing as us. But I don't know why.

OUR TREASURE GROTTO was hollowed out and lined with reinforced concrete by German soldiers during the Second World War. It lies facing the shipping lane; the Germans needed the position to attack and then to protect the approach to the town. They did a thorough, Germanic job and left behind a construction that is virtually inviolable from sea and invisible from land, and on which neither wind nor water have managed to scratch their traces in fifty years. Today it is used — at least we hope and believe so — only by us, when we are out on a treasure hunt.

You lead the way. That is to say, you walk behind and give me precise instructions, for as any experienced expedition leader knows, it is tactically important to have an advance guard. The entrance to the grotto lies hidden under a jutting outcrop of rock, and it is dark even before we have set foot inside. But we are well prepared. By the glow of a lighter I find the tallow candles that we have placed around the floor on previous visits and light them, and I am soon able to confirm that the grotto is suitably illuminated and free from villains. I walk out to you. You stand with one foot on top of your chest, as though on a lion you have just bagged, and listen as I make my report. Then in we go. This time you walk in front.

Deep inside the grotto a loose rock leans from the wall. You ease it out by the flickering light, which imparts an eerie life to our shadows, but you pay them no mind. Then you stick your hand inside and presently your whole arm. You don't spend a second worrying about scorpions and snakes, and ...

— Yes, I know, Gabriel, spending is something you do with money, but believe me, you can also spend time.

... and with a face that lights up in surprise and joy, outshining the flames, you pull out a fist full of pearls and gold chains and coins and coloured gemstones.

— Look what I found, Dad! Isn't it fantastic?

And then at once an afterthought that you need to have clarified:

— Do you think they're genuine?

WHAT IS A GENUINE TREASURE?

I could begin by throwing a question back at you:

— What does it mean, genuine?

You would simply tell me to stop asking stupid questions:

— Everybody knows what genuine means! It means things that aren't fake, things are real. Diamonds, for example.

And yet I might insist:

— Yes, but pine cones and mussels are real. Does that mean they're genuine?

You would immediately dismiss this:

—But they aren't rare!

— Maybe not — but what if in the whole world there was only one pine cone?

You would have to think about that for a few moments, and reply with a question of your own:

— Would that make it valuable?

— Yes, because if enough people wanted a pine cone, and in the whole wide world there was only one, then it would be very valuable.

You'd think a good deal more before trumping me:

— No, because genuine treasures actually exist, and only one pine cone doesn't, and so it can't be genuine!

WHAT IS A GENUINE TREASURE?

You have several criteria, but what is common to most of what you call genuine is that it must be created in and by nature, not by people. Among metals, you dismiss steel and brass. The main metals should also — if they are to be approved by you — have a carat stamp, or demonstrably be so old that age makes them rare and therefore valuable. In questions of valuation you adhere uncompromisingly to the gold standard — a treasure that cannot in principle be exchanged for gold does not deserve to be called a treasure. You give plated and gilded objects the benefit of the doubt, if they look good, but not if they show any signs of verdigris or rust.

Precious stones must above all be precious. However, here we are in murky waters, for apart from the obvious ones — diamonds, rubies, emeralds, turquoises, and sapphires — there are many types of stones that can *seem* precious without definitely being so. Agate, opal, amber, amethyst, tiger's eyes, rodomite, obsidian, jade … who could say with certainty if they are all precious and therefore genuine and valuable and rare? On this score you lack an authoritative reference book. Crystals are an especially tricky case, and you can never quite get to the bottom of it. Rock crystals are genuine, as is pink quartz from Argentina, but on the other hand you've learned that crystals are the building blocks in everything from salt to snowflakes, and it confuses you, for that has nothing to do with treasures. Crystal balls, on the other hand, and a crystal glass that rings against a damp finger drawn round the rim are genuine, even though they are not found in nature. They are at least valuable. Porcelain too, if it is thin enough. And fossils and corals, for they are millions of years old and so must be valuable.

As for materials and rugs, you accept only velvet and silk, *genuine* silk, mind you, unless some more common material has woven threads of gold or silver. It's hard for you to understand why Persian rugs should be collectible — they're just made of wool, and wool is as common as pine cones, even if it occurs in nature and consequently can't be valuable.

You have little time for things made of leather, but hides and furs are treasures, including sheepskin and goatskin; but the finest one you have is a reindeer hide, and you dream of a tiger skin. Your reasoning here is a little diffuse and above all related to the fact that furs are soft to the touch, and that kings and emperors usually go around wrapped in the skin of some animal. This criterion — pure luxury — is the most recent addition. Among other things it led you to suggest, when our old car finally had to be junked, that now we should get ourselves a limousine.

— Or a normal car, if you can't afford it, only make sure it's *long*, as you put it.

You have, thank goodness, not yet begun to take an interest in antiques, though you count Buddha statues, pill boxes, Egyptian scarabs, and miniature Turkish sabres as treasures, though they are made by people and of brass, and don't even have real jewels inlaid in them. Pearls too, it goes without saying, and shells and conches, but they should preferably be overlaid with mother-of-pearl, or come from a sufficiently distant ocean, or be big enough.

Size is otherwise not an absolute condition. You made that clear after we had been to see the silver mines in Kongsberg, and among other things I had bought you a lovely amethyst. You were perfectly happy and had no need at all of something bigger. Or as you put it during dinner at the camping site that evening:

— Hey, Dad?

— Yes?

— If — and I only mean *if* — we'd bought an amethyst in Kongsberg that was much, much bigger than the one I got, it wouldn't have made any difference. I would just have kept it.

— OF COURSE, I REPLY.

— Of course they're genuine. Why would anyone take the trouble to hide treasures deep inside a secret grotto if they weren't genuine?

This chain of reasoning appeals to you, and you agree at once. Carefully, you carry the newly discovered treasures out in the daylight to examine them, check that they're undamaged and complete, and nod your head in acknowledgement. We were pretty lucky today.

Then you open your chest. You lay the latest treasures inside separately and cover them over with a silk rag. I suggest we should perhaps take some of your other treasures and hide them, now that we've been lucky enough to discover this secret grotto. That seems a great idea to you, and you begin to pick out precious stones and pearls, bracelets and coins. But then you hesitate, put the agate back inside the chest, and choose a plainer crystal.

— Because what if some mean and *dishonest* pirates come and steal my agate?

The choice made, we carry the treasures into the grotto, and you place them deep down in the hollow space at the back, before wedging the rock back into place. We blow out the candles, each take hold of the handle on our side of the chest, and set out for the boat and the sail home.

Treasure Island gradually disappears in the evening mist behind us. You sit in your usual seat in the bow and keep a lookout for unknown shores. Suddenly you turn toward me and shout, so that I can hear you above the drone of the motor:

— Hey, Dad?

— Yes? I shout back.

— I know we'll have to wait and see, but what do you think? Do you think maybe we'll find some treasures next time we go to the grotto?

CHAPTER EIGHT

*W*inter is on its way. It's cold and dark and wet, so Mom and I have a suggestion:

That party you talk about so often, Gabriel, let's have it! Let's invite the whole family and make your favourite food, dessert too, and let's decorate for a feast! Let's invite everybody, twenty-three people big and small, and rig up a long table all the way through the living room for everyone to sit around. Let's make a fire, and buy flowers, and light candles in brightly polished candlesticks, and place burning torches outside. Let's set the table with our finest china, silver, and crystal, and dress up in our best clothes. Let's have a banquet!

You exult, even though a party, at least in principle, implies that you have to help vacuum and wash and tidy your room. You love having a party, having the house full of people, especially the family, for you feel safe and happy when you're surrounded by the people who define you, who frame you and who unconditionally — as you take for granted — love you, because they appear as a seamless extension of Mom and Dad.

First we have to get the invitations off to the ones who live farthest away: Aunt Ingeborg in Geneva, Aunt Liv in Los Angeles, Granny and Granddad in Oslo, and Uncle Trygve in the North Sea. It doesn't matter that they'll have to travel a long way and that it's expensive, because your piggy bank is full of money and you can buy them tickets, you can even buy a whole *private* jet that they can sit and relax in and eat and watch films. The others too will get invitations — Grandma and Grandpa, Kai Henrik and Kristina and their gang, Alexander and Annette, Aunt Bessie and the kids, and Deborah — but they don't live that far away, so they can drive their cars or take the bus. And Balder and Tina and Balthazar, though of course dogs and cats and roosters can't read, so we don't need to make invitations for them, nor for the rabbits or the guinea pig that died. And we who live here, we surely don't need invitations — although, why not? Let's make some for ourselves too, Mom and Victoria, Dad and Gabriel, that way it'll be the same for everybody.

What about the food? What shall we serve? Not fish, at any rate! How about chicken soup? No, they once tried to make that at school, but it didn't work out, you recall, because there was no chicken in the soup, it had flown away. It'll have to be spaghetti, your favourite, with meat and tomato sauce and basil and oregano and bay leaves and stuff, only we don't eat the bay leaves. And a salad, of course, but not with tuna fish. And pannacotta for dessert, with strawberry jam! And cakes and cream buns. And an appetizer — or no, let's not bother, otherwise we'll get so full we might not have room for dessert.

YOU LOOK FORWARD TO IT. You look forward to it with a great and unabashed sincerity that is always a pleasure to witness. But you don't see. You have no idea, no suspicion that this party of yours, which we've promised you, and which we will have, is not something we look forward to. Because there are times, Gabriel, when we're so unspeakably tired. There are times when we don't know if we can cope.

I have to say this as it is, my friend, because otherwise I'd be lying, and we won't do that to each other, we've promised. I have to tell you that we feel it's hard, Mom and I. Sometimes we feel it's so hard that we almost can't take any more, because we're exhausted and just want to give up. You occupy every hour of our waking lives — and often the nights too — with demands and expectations that even you find complicated and inscrutable, and that we don't always have the strength to understand, far less meet. You demand and you insist, but we don't always have any more to give — of high spirits when you're sulking and depressed, of desire to do things and go places when you're bored and nagging, of patience to accompany you through your mental labyrinths when you get lost, of surplus energy to help you when you can't find your way out and get stuck and everything goes black, and you yell and punch and kick and bite and shove and smash, when you've been howling and screaming all day, from the moment you woke up, no matter what we've tried to say or do, until you fall asleep late at night, exhausted by your own unfathomable rage.

Then we sometimes get so tired, Gabriel, so full of despair that we can't even sleep. And so we vent our despair on the other, quarrel and blame, turn silent, cold backs on each other, say ugly and hurtful things that we might not mean but feel a need to mean, and we have to say them to someone, and there isn't anyone else to say them to. And it gets late, but we can't face the thought of going to bed with all this, at least not together, even though we know that one of us has to get up with you, you wake up at first light regardless of how long you've slept, and then that too becomes a discussion, and one of us volunteers in a way that makes the other feel guilt, yet more guilt, we never seem to get enough.

And because you've had so little sleep you're bad-tempered and grumpy from the moment you open your eyes, and you waste time and won't wear the trousers I've found for you, and you don't like the breakfast spreads and throw your slice of bread at Victoria, because she's grumpy in the morning too and has just tossed off some sarcasm at you, and the jam splashes all over the table and the wall, and finally I explode in a rage that I cannot and don't even want to control, because this is too much. I give you both a thorough scolding with ugly and unfair words, and Victoria shrieks that she can't stand any more of this madhouse, this insane family, and runs off weeping through the door and forgets to take her lunch pack, and you're howling because you don't understand why everyone is so angry, and Mom wakes and gets up, even though it's her day off, and she comes in and hisses at me with contempt in her voice, because she can't or won't control herself either, that I'm behaving worse than a little child, and she comforts you and tries to rescue the start of this sad day, and I don't know what to do with all my dreadful conscience, I don't know what to do with myself, so I go into my study and close the door and try to sit completely still and do nothing at all.

Then the taxi arrives and it pains me, my whole body aches, because I can't just let you go after this, but in the hallway you won't even look at me, you just sniffle and tell Mom that you think I'm stupid, that you want another dad, and Mom dutifully says that's no way to talk, you don't mean that, and she follows you out, and you don't even hear my faint, guilt-laden attempt to shout sorry and goodbye.

Days like this, Gabriel, drain us just as much as you. And they don't just drain our strength; they also empty the house of everything that makes it a home, love and trust, goodwill and joy. Days like this threaten us, and if there are too many of them in a row, they fill us to the brim with a need and a desire to flee, to move, to live another life. Even though we know that there is no other life. What would that be? A divorce, a broken home? The great defeat, a betrayal of you and Victoria, of ourselves and of each other? It's a thought we back away from, refuse to think through, but sometimes we give way to temptation and think it anyway. When we see nothing but exhaustion and aversion and ashes in each other's faces, and imagine that the world out there is full of enticing vitality and playful smiles, full of other lives than this. Then it's sometimes best, after all, to go away for a few days, Mom to a close girlfriend or to some unnecessary seminar in another town, me to an old friend who doesn't ask questions or a quiet hotel room in Oslo. So that afterwards it will be possible to come back home, to you and to Victoria and to the other one, who has held the fort and made the flight possible, and who has also had a chance to be alone. We've talked about this,

Mom and I, and we agree that we couldn't have made it together without being so much apart.

But of all this you know nothing. Nor do you know about Victoria, how difficult she has found it. Not only to be dethroned as a princess because a little prince was born, but at times to feel neglected and ignored because it was you who needed and got all the attention. How difficult it has been for her to understand that her sweet, lovely little brother wasn't like other sweet, lovely little brothers, how afraid she has been of this that made you different and that no one, not even Mom and Dad, could explain to her, because they didn't understand it themselves. How ashamed she has been when you've embarrassed her and made her feel awkward in front of her pals at school and her boyfriends. How she has fought tooth and nail out there to defend you if anyone gave even a hint of criticism or made a sarcastic remark. How she has brought boys home with her to test them, and rejected them without a second thought if they failed, if they couldn't deal with you, or dealt with you in the wrong way, cocky and immature, because she saw in your eyes that you didn't like them and therefore she couldn't respect them.

You only know that she loves you, boundlessly, that she is on your side in the world, and that happiness is a cuddle with her on the sofa, and perhaps, perhaps to be allowed to sleep with her in her bed. You have a mother and sister who love strongly and unconditionally, Gabriel, because the Lord was reckless and prodigal with love the day he created them, and you have me.

AND HERE YOU HAVE the rest of the family!

First, a little shaky on their feet but with an imperious indifference toward the body's infirmities, Grandpa and Grandma make their entry — Sonja and Harald, as they're called. It's a standing joke, but (yes, I know you don't understand how a joke can stand, but we'll let that lie for the moment) it's not their fault they have the same names as the King and Queen of Norway. Right behind them in the crush by the front door come the excited youngsters, Malin, Michelle, and Jeffrey, and after them, with considerably less impatience, your big brothers with wife and girlfriend, and the other young ones. Bessie and Deborah make up the rear, laden with plates of cake. The long-distance travellers that you're bringing over in your own private jet won't arrive for another half-hour yet.

You stand in the doorway and are supposed to greet and welcome everyone, but then you don't have the time. You've got a decorated banquet table to show off, you've got treasures on display for all to see, and dessert glasses with pannacotta in the fridge, and the guinea pig that died. Before the guests have taken off their overcoats you're on your way to the table, and before the last ones have arrived your mind is on the cakes.

Your time is faster than ours, Gabriel. It gets done with things quicker, its content needs refilling more frequently than ours. To a certain extent it's because you're a child and lack the adults' patience to wait, but mostly it's because your empirical time is somehow out of sync with the time of what fills it. You concentrate on people, objects, and events with a rhythm and intensity that are different from most other children's and adults'. I see it when you dance, I see it when you open presents on your birthday, when you play, eat, and dress yourself. I see how your attentive time rushes ahead, or stretches across slow eternities — how it almost never coincides with our empirical time when we dance or eat or get dressed in the morning.

But who can take your time away from you? Who can say that it's wrong? Our use of time is not ruled by laws, only by habits, but because we so easily make our habits universally valid, we forget that time has many speeds, and that your sense of time drives your attention at a tempo that is different from ours. We forget that a glance is enough for you in situations that to us seem to call for a half-hour's deliberation, and that to you an hour might seem barely adequate for something that we're done with in five minutes. When you ask me, as you often do, how long it is until something you're either dreading or looking forward to, you really only want to know whether it will be today, or if you'll have to sleep one or more nights first. A quarter of an hour or five hours, five days or two weeks, these are abstractions that mean nothing to you. On the other hand, you can relate to "When you get home from school," or "when it gets dark," or "after the summer holidays," even though you always find it unreasonably soon or impossibly far off.

I look at the guests filling the house and I look at you, and I see that this gathering operates with two times that are in many ways incompatible. Once more I feel an anxiety about how this evening will turn out — as I did this morning when you woke us up before dawn, draped from head to toe in silk, velvet, and furs, all dressed up and ready for the party.

THE YOUNG ONES — whom I must remind myself to regard as adults, they're in their twenties, after all, and have children themselves — rapidly disappear down into the library for a smoke. You tag along, having so much to tell these big brothers, whom you admire and want to be admired by, so much to share with them. But they've got their own things to talk and gossip about, jobs and friends, strained finances and problems they don't want you to hear about. I know this, and I bring you back up before you start demanding something they don't have the energy to give you.

Up in the living room it's cozy, the candles are lit and

reflected light glints in the newly polished silver. From the cooking pots come smells of tomato and herbs and oil, and Grandma and your cousin Kristin Isabel are sitting there rocking Deborah's newborn baby in their laps. The baby is lovely, you think so too, and want to hold and cuddle her. Of course, they say, just be careful. But you're too much, you're too big and overwhelming, and little Monica begins to cry in your arms. You can see no reason for this, all you've done is be good and kind, and you make it clear that this is a stupid baby.

— No, Gabriel, we mustn't say things like that, you don't mean it, comes the mild rebuke from the group of women on the sofa, and that provokes you, because of course you meant it, otherwise you wouldn't have said it! Your voice rises in tone and pitch with each word of your sentence, and the concluding exclamation mark is chiselled in angry wrinkles between your eyes. Mom enters from the kitchen in time to defuse the situation, and suggests that you go have a chat with Grandpa.

He sits discussing safety routines and weather prospects for the winter with William, your cousin, who has started work on a ferry boat in the north of the county. You lean up against Grandpa's comfy body, want to be babied a bit yourself, and his big fist rests upon your head, and it's safe and pleasant when he strokes you. But he continues talking to William about things you don't understand, and you want more, you want to cuddle him and creep up into his lap and press your nose into the hollow of his neck even though you're a big boy, and he lets it happen, lets you climb and crawl on his mountainous body, but then that too gets to be too much. He lifts you down and you understand; you manage to check yourself, not to protest and make it embarrassing, make people think you're a little baby. You demonstratively pull your arm out of his hand and turn to leave, but in your haste you step on Balder's tail. He's lying on the floor and is so dark against it you can't see him. He yelps so loudly that even Victoria looks up from her mobile phone, and little Malin is afraid, and you run over to comfort her, but then you see that it's your treasures she's sitting and playing with on the rug. At that point, fortunately, the doorbell rings.

Your private jet has landed and the last guests arrive. Granddad immediately has to promise to tell you a bedtime fairy story; you can hardly wait for the continuation of what you heard in the summer when we visited them at their holiday home. Granny has brought a little present, and so have Aunt Liv and Aunt Ingeborg. It's true that you haven't seen any of them for a long time, but the presents you've never seen at all, so we have to realize that they're more important than telling how you're doing at school, or agreeing that yes, indeed, you really are a big boy now. Everyone smiles at this, and then they proceed into the living room to say hello to the others, and how nice it was last time we met, it must have been, can it really be, good grief how time flies.

In the kitchen, everything is ready. I ask your sister to tear herself away from her mobile for a moment and give the word to those sitting in the library. She's about to ignore the request, then registers that Granny is following the scene, and since she's the one who sends the monthly envelopes that pay the phone bill, Victoria jumps up and disappears down the corridor. Seconds later she's back, exasperated, but understanding in the way she shakes her head and rolls her eyes, and signals for me to come. I know that look, and I follow her. From the corridor she points into the toilet, and there you sit, on the floor, with the contents of your mother's makeup bag strewn around you, your face transformed into an extravaganza of lipstick, mascara, and cream in red, black, and white. With half a tin of gel you've styled your hair into a pyramid. A loud, angry NO is on its way out of my mouth, but I manage to swallow it, replace it with a milder rebuke about how Mom is going to be sad and sorry, and begin to wash and clean you up. Most of the abomination is water-resistant, and by the time I'm finished and we go in to take our places you still look like you have some sinister skin disease, but that can't be helped. We've seen worse in this house before.

That isn't true of everyone sitting around the table, but no one says anything. Then they smile nevertheless and say well, well, we've all been children once, no getting away from that, I remember so clearly — and with that Grandma embarks on a tale about one of the many times when little Henni and her best friend had got up to some mischief you just wouldn't believe, and Granny nods meaningfully and adds, pointing at me, that him there, he wasn't such an easy lad either, trust me, and soon the whole table is buzzing with reminiscences and confessions of long ago. In moments of fumbling uncertainty like this it's often reassuring to take refuge in the past, in what, thank God, ended well, though for a while there we thought — because things that happened back then are no longer dangerous and don't count in the same way, because sometimes it's helpful to recall memories of bad things that happened in childhood since, beside making good stories, they reassure us that everything, without exception, passes.

While this collective and unbridled confession proceeds, and even Victoria and Alexander and Kai Henrik find inspiration and encouragement to admit to misdemeanours and infringements that Mom and I have neither heard of nor wish to know about, I look at you. You sit bent over your plate, your face and the spaghetti sauce like reflections of each other, apparently consumed by the food you're bolting down. But your whole body tells me that you hear each word that's being said, and that you're having trouble dealing with them. They muddy your picture of reality, these things you hear about Mom and me and Granddad and the others, and which everyone around the table just smiles and laughs at. Here, too many boundaries are being violated simultaneously — the gap between right and wrong; the difference between what you know you're allowed to do, and what you've been told you should be ashamed of and apologize for; the chasm between adults who know and children who haven't learned; the distinction between scolding and laughter; the fine and often imperceptible line between laughing at something that's funny and laughing at something that's stupid. You can't get any of these sums to add up. Nothing seems to be as you've learned it should be and usually is.

Perhaps it occurs to you, in an attempt to understand, that tonight there are no rules, or that none of them apply? Is that why you abruptly sit up straight and launch into a piercing sentence that contains all the ugliest words you know, and that soon contains no words at all, just atonal sounds, while you roll your eyes up into your forehead and plaster spaghetti from your plate into your hair and onto your face and clothes? Is it because this party was supposed to be yours and no one is talking with you or about you? Because there are, after all, too many people and voices, and too much noise? Because you feel offended without knowing why, and are therefore confused? Is that why you grab the glass on your right and, lightning quick, before anyone can react, the glass on your left, and with a sheepish look that pretends not to see what the hands are getting up to, empty them both into the pasta bowl?

— Gabriel!

Mom slaps your hand and takes you by the arm to lead you from the table, but it's too late now. There's no way back now, you're gone, furious and shocked, and you bite the joint of her thumb and kick yourself free and run off, and we hear shrieking and swearing from the corridor, and the front door closing with a bang.

Then all is still. I look at our large family seated around the table, I see how they try, a little embarrassed, to disguise their upset and outrage, and it strikes me that I've almost forgotten what it means to be upset and outraged. All I feel is grief, a grief that makes me nauseous and makes me want to close my eyes and let go.

Slowly the table comes back to life. Granny and Grandma start clearing away, carrying out, rinsing and loading the dishwasher, as if to wash clean the whole meal. And now everybody wants to help, because they must do something, get the evening back on track by performing practical tasks. Little Malin, three years old, wants to know why Uncle Gabriel was so angry, but they hush her and tell her to go off and play. The young, who strictly speaking are adults, probably want to laugh more than anything, it's so crazy, but they don't do so here. They say they're going for a smoke and head off down to the library. Victoria has a telephone to address, and Grandpa and Granddad sit on the sofa and make conversation about something.

Finally, Mom and I sit alone at the table. We look at each

other and know that this is something we two have to live with, this is something no one else can understand or help us with, and this certainty is so strong and so necessary that we have to stand up and hold each other long and hard. Then we go, she out to the grandmothers in the kitchen, and me out into the night, to you.

WINTER IS ON ITS WAY. It's cold and dark, and you've run off. I didn't follow you straightaway, for I know that you need your time after a scene such as this. You need to be alone for the time it takes, while shattered chains of thought slowly link themselves together again, enabling you to create a sort of order that makes it possible for you to carry on thinking. But I'm freezing already, and all you were wearing when you disappeared was a shirt and no shoes.

Where shall I search for you? How shall I find you?

I start walking along the gravel path. There's no point in calling for you — even if you hear me over the wind, you won't answer. In the place you are now, it's all the rest of us who are guilty, we're the ones who started it, and the only one to feel sorry for is you. An answer to my call would be an admission, yet another humiliation. Wherever you are, you want to be found like a treasure.

Walking along casting purposeless glances into the night, I can't think clearly. I try to search, but at the same time I replay over and over again a recording of what happened, and rehearse what sentences to use when I find you. An ugly little thought-demon wants me to contemplate the very worst, that despair has driven you down to the sea to give up completely, and for a moment I'm terrified, but then immediately I get furious, warm, and strong, and I crush every little devil beneath my heel, crunch the gravel and these satanic skulls, smash every bone in the body of everyone who would dare to hurt my boy.

Then I turn, suddenly calm again, leave this meaningless battlefield and walk back toward the house. The guests and the party and the laughter light up the windows, but the light lies, for a great emptiness fills this house, an absence that takes up more space than all the people and all the objects and all the dreams.

I walk into the garden, stepping on wet winter grass, and I stop and look at the tree that stretches its rheumatic witch limbs toward the east, just about distinguishing them in black on black, and then I discover you, the outline of your body, kneeling and curved, folded into itself, on the ground inside the rabbit hutch.

You've sensed me; I know that without knowing. I walk over and sit down cross-legged outside the chicken wire that I don't see, only feel as an icy imprint on my forehead when I bend forward. You're not crying; you sit quite still. The shadows of four small rabbits scurry around you.

— My boy, I say.

— Yes, you say.

I stand up and open the hutch cover and wriggle inside, sit down in front of you. In the darkness your face is Indian and pirate, clown and wizard, but the eyes are Gabriel, large and beautiful and filled with prayer.

— Dad, you say.

— Yes, I say.

We hold each other, hold tightly on to the only thing that can help us, the other, and the rabbits lie down flat on the ground and the wind holds its breath.

— It was a stupid party, you say.

— Yes, I say.

And then you lower your gaze to the ground, modestly and gently, as though it were too heavy even for the globe itself to bear, and whisper:

— Do you think Granddad will still tell me that fairy story?

CHAPTER NINE

*W*hen people first chose to settle here, I imagine that it was because the landscape spoke to them as it sometimes speaks to us. They didn't have to stay here, they could have continued northward, or inland, or gone south, they could have set sail and perhaps discovered America. But they didn't. They stopped, they looked around and listened, and what they saw and heard told them that they had arrived.

I don't know what it was that the rocky knolls and the grass and the waves said to them, or what language they spoke. Perhaps it was a beautiful song the people heard, perhaps it was a silence like they'd never experienced before. Perhaps it was a message from their Creator that danger threatened in every direction and that they had no option but to stay here. It's also possible that the light here drove the shadows from their hearts and in their place left a sparkling promise of happiness and freedom.

Perhaps all this, but it was surely the wind too, that blew them full of a riddle they would have to live ten thousand years to solve, while they patiently ploughed the fields and the ocean, sowed seed and bait, harvested corn and salmon. And this riddle is so huge that it encompasses all they have ploughed and sown and harvested, and the fields and the ocean and all they are and ever can be, and that itself is the solution, that is the answer they have left behind.

This is your landscape, Gabriel. Here you shall encounter the riddle yourself, and perhaps find your own answers, since ours are usually insufficient for you.

EVERYTHING IS LANGUAGE. Language gives names to all things, and therefore you can acquire them through language. Acquiring is not the same as possessing, it's more like mastering, and since you can't possess all things, you can master them with the help of language. This is something you've understood by yourself. You find it just as self-evident that your world grows bigger the more things you can give a name to, as the fact that there is less white left on the drawing paper the more pencil lines you draw and the more strokes you make with the paintbrush.

This you know, regardless of how difficult language is, of how it's guided by rules that have neither overt reason nor evident logic. We've talked about this, and they make you laugh, all the strange thoughts one can have about language. For example, that there is no good reason why a glass can't be called a horse, or a sweater. You laugh, but you understand it, because although our dog is named Balder he might just as well have been called Rufsen or Tinka. Moreover there are many dogs named Balder, and some people too, so a name is just something we decide upon, it isn't the glass, or the horse, or Balder. But it's fun to see the look on Mom's face when you ask her for a horse of orange juice.

All the same, it's a big jump from understanding something, for example, that the words in language are arbitrary, that they might easily have been different, the way they are in other languages — to accepting without protest that this is simply the way it is, not to demand some better explanation or rationale. A jump like that involves a transgression of your conception of independence that you are usually reluctant to undertake. It's almost like a jump from equality to subordination.

— I know that's how it is, you say, — but I don't understand why it *has* to be like that *always*. Why can't I be allowed to think what I want?

And straightaway we're into one of those endless conversations in which your contributions are limited to: Yes, but why?

And yet you submitted without more ado to the peculiarities of language, like grass to wind and wave to beach. Was it perhaps because you knew intuitively that you needed language in order to pose questions about everything else? Or did you maybe find a secret symmetry, some invisible logic that appealed to you, in what to us seems a quite arbitrary concurrence between the world and the words we use to animate it by giving names to all things? Or — as I suspect every now and then — was it simply that the hunter and the collector in you discovered early that in language you had stumbled upon the richest treasure chest of them all?

It isn't important. The wind doesn't ask why the grass bends as though bowing, it just blows on. Nor does language want to know why it makes the world comprehensible; it just gives you more to comprehend.

THE LANDSCAPE OUT HERE is as big as language. In all directions the sky stretches into eternity, the ocean foams and breaks against coasts where it has other and unknown names, islands and skerries have roots deep in the earth and in time that was long before time began, and the wind, and all the innumerable things that grow because they are small and demand little, just a name that is unlike all other names, in order to exist.

The landscape out here is more precise than other landscapes in forests and mountains. It has so much space at its disposal, so much elbow room that we would have got lost in it if we didn't know exactly what it was called and where we therefore belong. It has so much weather to endure, the landscape out here, such powerful forces that we might have lost ourselves in it had we not had the names to cling to — one name in fog, another in storm, and many more in blinding sun and ice-cold moonlight, and nights that are so black you can touch them.

This is no landscape for tourists. It's a landscape to settle in, or to move on from, for one has to work one's way into it with reverence and patience, knoll for knoll, wave for wave, wind for wind. It's a tough landscape that wears down all opposition and survives every assault, for it lies so limitlessly open and exposed that it's unshakeable and impenetrable. It's a landscape of shifting otherness, hour by hour, day by day, and yet always, to the point of melancholy, the same.

It's a landscape that often reminds me of you, Gabriel. It's your kind of landscape.

IF ONLY WORDS had been enough!

But they are not, because words also need to have a home somewhere, they need a circumstance, a context within which to order themselves. Like grass and people, words need a place of their own, or else they become placeless, and then they lose their meaning and we can't understand them.

This too you know. I can't teach you anything about how words need to belong either, for you know about it in the way one simply knows that certain things are impossible, or right, or necessary like air and blood, inexorable as the ebb and flow of the tides. You know that words must have a fixed place that is theirs and no one else's, but you know it so well that at times it seems a crippling insight — a knowledge you have elevated to a truth, to some law of nature that you dare not, cannot, break for fear of disturbing an order, a system, a context only you can see and that has made you its slave. At times your dependence on context is frightening.

One day as we were seated around the dinner table, Victoria asked permission to do something. I can't remember exactly what, but anyway, our answer was a firm and clear no. To which her response, with exaggerated gestures, was:

—*Mamma mia!*

You were instantly gripped by a violent and furious confusion, you screamed and wept, and then you lay down on the sofa and hid your head beneath a cushion, as though to hide your impotence. We didn't understand what had happened, had no means to follow you into the labyrinth and escort you back, for we had no idea of the cause of your reaction. Only later, when you had calmed down, did it emerge that it was Victoria's outburst: she had used the expression *Mamma mia* wrongly. You knew the ABBA song, and that expression belonged there and nowhere else. By using it to emphasize her frustration with us, Victoria had broken your law governing the fixed context of all words, and this transgression violated your understanding of language in a way that was unacceptable to you. For you, the context of words is as holy and sacrosanct as their meaning.

YOU KNOW MANY, MANY WORDS, Gabriel. You know what they mean, the difference between them down to the slightest nuance, and you use them meticulously, diligently, and cautiously, and almost never get them mixed up. Synonyms aren't for you interchangeable words that have the same meaning; they are independent words and mean different things that only resemble each other. No word can mean exactly the same as another, for in a specific context all things can have only one word. Otherwise language would be nothing but what you call chaos and jumble, and impossible to use. For you, each individual word has an intrinsic value precisely because it cannot and should not be confused with any other.

You use words as specialized tools. When you talk, you practise precision mechanics. You can embark on a sentence, a complicated, many-layered piece of reasoning, but near the end you'll often stop and reconsider, shake your head and say no, no, no, that's not what I meant, and then start all over again in order to replace a word in the middle with one that is a little more precise and appropriate to the context. You're like a writer who, having completed a whole page on the machine, discovers a typo in the middle and therefore tears the page out of the typewriter, throws it away and starts anew because he can't bear to see a small, insignificant mistake spoil the textual image. Had you been a wind blowing across a desert, you would have turned back and blown all over again if a single grain of sand you'd swept over on your way had rolled too far, or not far enough.

In many ways, Gabriel, it's a gift to master words and their meanings individually and in context the way you do. It's a gift that has also brought me great pleasure. I, who for many years have earned a living working with language and thought I knew a good deal about it, have learned more about the value and need for precision and nuance by following your process of linguistic maturation than from most of the books I have read. Because you never content yourself with an approximate answer, you won't put up with sentences that are merely there or thereabouts, that are not the exact, optimal, and literal expression of what you want to say.

But unfortunately language isn't always literal, no more than words are always faithful to the context in which you first encountered them. Language cannot always be literal, because then we wouldn't be able to develop and change and enrich it by forming new words and adjusting the meaning of the old ones. Language is, moreover, a toy as well as a tool. Will you ever be able to accommodate that? Will you manage to come to terms with the fact that language can be used for more than giving things the right name in the right contexts, that it can also be used to play with the things and the contexts, to joke and to fool about with? That it is quite possible to say something in a way that turns its meaning into the opposite of what one is actually saying? That words can be lifted from their contexts and placed in others, thus acquiring new, unexpected, and amusing meanings? That it is possible to make pictures with words just as one does with colours and pencils, and that the finest pictures are often the result of mixing words to make new ones, just as you mix colours? That it's okay to experiment, and that a failed word image can be thrown away just like a drawing you haven't got right?

Now and then you tell us jokes that you've heard at school and expect us to laugh at them, but you do not laugh yourself. Or you laugh without laughing, because you've understood that jokes are to be laughed at. Nor do you laugh at word games, although you sometimes play them yourself, innocently, and unintentionally, as when Victoria told you she was going to the kiosk to buy a ticket for the Viking lottery, and asked if you wanted to go with her. You didn't reply at once; first you had to know:

— Does that mean I can win coins from the Viking Age?

Will you learn to play and joke with words? The landscape plays with us all the time. The clouds are faces and scary animals, but they don't stop being clouds. The sea is glittering gold in the sunset, but it doesn't stop being the sea. The tree in the garden has gnarled witch's claws and an eagle has landed on the outermost islet, but you know that what you see are dry branches and a pointed rock. Words aren't dangerous to play with, Gabriel; they retain their usual meanings even though from time to time we lend them other new and strange meanings. It doesn't matter if you sometimes want to drink a horse or a sweater of orange juice — that doesn't stop the glass from being a glass.

THE LANDSCAPE OUT HERE talks to us, but it can also be read, almost like our palms. Wherever you look, memories are etched into it like writing. You read a minor clause in the landscape's diary when you turn over a stone on the ground and the exposed pallor tells you how long it has been lying there, and you gulp down entire chapters each time you let your gaze sweep over the skerries' polished grey-black tide line. Moment by moment the wind spells the weather in water and grass, and the sun never stops counting the days. The landscape keeps a careful log in its elegant hand, so that we can read about what has been and prepare ourselves for what is to come, so that we may know where we are and determine whether we have any reason to be here. Sometimes I picture the landscape as a written warning.

You who talk and talk, why have you hesitated so long to read and write? The letters, which are so orderly, which each have their own sound, unlike all other sounds, and which in all conceivable contexts — in every word — have their fixed, unchanging places. For a long time you've known all the letters, you've know the sounds they stand for, and you've been aware that when you put one sound after another they turn into words and sentences. Is it because you couldn't believe it was that easy? That there had to be some aspect of the art of reading and writing you hadn't understood? Is that why you insisted for so long that you couldn't do it? Even though you sometimes, at moments when you'd forgotten that you couldn't, actually read — a sign, a newspaper headline, an advertising bill. Given your keenness to learn, and your infinite curiosity, and all the questions you knew there were answers to in books, your reluctance was a mystery. Yet another mystery.

But it turned out it was just me who didn't understand, or who forgot that you always need your own time to formulate your own justifications, that they must be irrefutable and that you must believe in them before you set about anything new. Eventually your curious aversion to fish proved to be of some use, for one day at the dinner table you brightly delivered a classic and unassailable piece of Gabriel-reasoning:

— Mom, now I understand it, now I know why I have to learn to read. Because if I'm sitting in a restaurant with my girlfriend and the waiter comes with the menu — if I can't read it then I'll just have to point, and what if he brings me fish soup!

And with that, almost overnight, you began reading everything you came across, be it in Norwegian, English, Spanish, or sloppy handwriting. And you took to writing — letters, notes, e-mails and messages. You discovered that writing could replace action, as on the day you came home from school and would neither say hello nor anything else but simply pressed a piece of paper into my hand and disappeared up into your room. *Ay-yam-so — angry-that — ay'm-steaming*, it said. When you came down a little later, you only needed to assure yourself that I'd read and understood the message for your good humour to be restored. And you write stories, sometimes from Indian mythology, which you find it easier to relate to than the abstractions of Christianity. I kept one of them, because it would hardly be possible to tell any story more concisely:

> *Ganesh is a god in India.*
> *Shiva chopped off ganesh's head.*
> *His mother was out of her mind with grief.*
> *The cervants had to travel the world and chop the*
> *   head off the first animal thay found.*
> *The first animal thay found was an elefent.*
> *Thay chopped off its head and put the head on*
> *   ganesh.*

All things have a beginning and an end. All things lead in the end to something other than themselves. Not even the words we use when we talk together can remain wholly and completely themselves when they leave one person's thoughts and enter into another's. We can never know, Gabriel, if we refer to the same thing when we say that a flower is "pretty" or that Mom is "kind." Maybe I mean that the flower's form is beautiful, and that Mom is generous, while you're thinking of the colour of the petals and are glad because Mom has given you permission to stay up late. That is why we now and then misunderstand one another; not because we don't understand, but because we understand in different ways.

This you find difficult. You find it difficult to think that it's possible to understand and not understand at the same time. It seems to defy common sense. You find it terrible whenever it dawns on you that you've misunderstood something we have said, and you find it intolerable when we misunderstand something you've said to us. Then you might get angry and depressed and give up, and not calm down until we finally, after repeated attempts, hit upon the exact meaning you intended us to understand. It's like when you in your haste can't find the one word you want to use — not one that's similar and means almost the same, but that precise one word — and become furious with yourself and with the language that lets you down. In such moments I want so much to tell you that misunderstandings aren't dangerous, that on the contrary they can be quite funny, that they can teach us new things, give us thoughts we wouldn't otherwise have.

But to you misunderstandings are dangerous. They create disorder and breaches in lines of thought you've laboriously linked into a precise utterance. Just as the landscape around you is only rain when it rains, and only sunshine in fair weather, you are wholly and completely present in each of your individual thoughts, consumed exclusively by each one and unwilling to mix them with others, to mess them up and invite misunderstanding. Then they crash, as you put it, and nothing good comes of it, just confusion and rage. Because then that which you probably depend on above all is threatened: logic.

All people depend on logic, on the belief that one thing has to happen before another can, that something comes first and something else comes next, and that everything follows from something else. Without logic we wouldn't be able to do even the most ordinary things, like putting on our shirt before our pullover, or taking the cork out of the bottle before pouring, and neither would we be able to understand the simplest things, such as other people feeling pain if we hit them. But there is a big and decisive difference between yours and other people's logic that often makes yours problematic, while for others it's only beneficial. It is a difficult difference, but an important one.

For Mom and I and most other people, logic is a way of thinking we use to create and maintain order in things, to avoid doing things in the wrong order, to understand how things are connected. But for you it's different. For you, logic is not just a way of thinking; it's a kind of quality inherent in all things, regardless of how we otherwise think of them. You regard logical structures as a necessity, but because you perceive them as an unavoidable part of the nature of all things, not because they're tools you feel necessary to make use of. That's why your respect for logic is so limitless and compulsive — because it's coincident with your understanding of the world. That's also why logical breaches, transgressions of the laws of logic, appear so terrible and intolerable to you — because they seem like breaches in the very order that, in your eyes, sustains the world and makes it comprehensible. A wise Danish man of science once said to a student something he might as well have said to you: You don't think, you're just logical.

There is only one exception: no matter how logical you are in all your considerations, you seem unwilling or unable to see that there exists a chain of cause and effect between your own actions and the reactions they can provoke in others, whether they be strangers, friends, or family. When you do something that makes others angry or sad, you choose — in defiance of the instincts that otherwise rule you — to be illogically injured and lay the blame unilaterally on others. As soon as the question of blame has been resolved, always in your favour, you begin justifying your sense of injury, only this time with customary logical thoroughness. Like that time at school when you weren't having "a good day" and in the end the teacher had to hold you to prevent more kicking and punching and biting:

— Why did they have to hold me? Don't they understand that it was the other kids that made me angry? If they'd understood that then they would've done something about them and not needed to hold me, because then I wouldn't have been angry.

Often I have to admire your ability to think logically. When I'm tired and worn out or busy with something else and you ask some difficult question that would take a long time to give a proper answer to, I sometimes take the risk of provoking you with a quick, short version. When I do, you often remain there standing, your gaze utterly empty, while I return to whatever I was doing. You stand there so silent and absent that I forget you, forget your question, and am completely bowled over (yes, you can say that, even though you're nowhere near a bowling alley) when you start up:

— Right, now I understand. Because if...

And then you erect, carefully and patiently, a gigantic and complicated structure of logical inferences that, link by link, lead you to conclude that my quick and apparently strange answer must have been right.

On the other hand, it's a little frightening, this unconditional faith of yours that logical chains of cause and effect can and should explain everything. Because it's a faith that makes you easy to trick. As long as an explanation satisfies your demands for logical consistency, it can in fact easily end in an outright lie or a crude absurdity, for you seem more concerned with the explanation's inner logic than with the answer it eventually arrives at. I have to confess that I myself have tricked you at times by playing on your blind faith that if A equals B and B equals C, then A must necessarily also equal C. That isn't always true in everyday life, outside the universe of pure logic, but I have abused your faith on occasions when I found no other way to get you to accept a decision, a fact, or a point of view.

I admire you, Gabriel, and at the same time I feel sorry for you. You have a great and impressive talent for language and logic, and without it you would have been lost. Yet that same talent is also a major source of much of your confusion and frustration. It brings you happiness and it makes you unhappy, and you can't have the one without exposing yourself to the other.

FROM THE BED I HEAR your sister's stiletto heels out in the corridor, and Mom's voice asking you to bring me a cup of coffee. Then the creaking of the stairs beneath your feet as you take the short steps down to the bedroom, syncopated by the slam of the front door. Mom and Victoria are off to work and to school, and it's my turn to get up.

This happens every weekday when we have to get up and go out, but today nothing is usual. I see it in your smile even before you've put down the coffee cup on the bedside table.

— Good morning, Gabriel.

— Yeah, yeah, good morning, you reply, keen to get these ritual greetings, which you otherwise seem to like, out of the way as quickly as possible. Nor do you have time to creep into bed beside me as you usually do, or perhaps it doesn't even occur to you that this is what you usually do, every single morning. Instead you trip about on the floor, almost Latin in your gesturing, and explain that some sheep have got into our garden.

Shouldn't I do something? At least go out and take a look?

— They're standing there pooping!

I lie under the duvet, knowing that the date is April 1. You know it too, but your way of expressing yourself reveals that you also think you're alone in remembering that today it's all right "to joke."

A moment later I'm on my feet, busily indignant and worried, because sheep shit on the lawn is the worst thing there is. After a short tour of *inspection* around the garden, I turn to you with a questioning look about where all the sheep have gone, and the laughter you've been carrying inside comes bursting out as you shout:

— April Fool!

Your face lights up with joy, but I can see, from the way your eyes sort of seek out mine, and the way you suddenly stand stock still, that what you're looking for most of all is an acknowledgement that you've mastered this curious art of foolery. My apparent surprise and smiling annoyance at having fallen for the trick are all you need; now the morning can continue in its usual fashion, with dressing, breakfast, and packing of your satchel.

Still, you now know that I know what day it is, and I have a hunch that you're expecting a kind of payback. I choose a moment when you're standing at the top of the staircase, on the way down to fetch your jacket and shoes. With a hint of panic in my voice, I shout:

— Look out, Gabriel! There's a snake on the stairs!

You stand still with your back to me, as though you need time to digest this piece of information. Then you turn toward me and say, in an indulgent and almost patronizing way:

— But, Dad, surely you know there are no snakes in Norway? Did you perhaps mean an adder?

— Yes, I'm sorry. Of course I meant an adder. But you'd better watch out, it's lying right next to your feet!

As soon as the linguistic clarification is out of the way, you become terrified and yell Help! and come running toward me while you cast anxious glances at the reptile on the staircase. Not until my "April Fool!" breaks the spell do you calm down: now you've shown that you also master the dupe's role in the foolery.

All the same, what this scene shows me most clearly is your unshakeable faith in words as conveyors of unequivocal knowledge. Even in the middle of an April Fool's joke, with both of us doing our best to pretend to trick and be tricked, you take time to interrupt the game with a correction: a snake must not be confused with an adder. You won't even let me joke with the wrong word.

This unconditional faith in the singularity of words, which at times can make you so superior and masterly, is at other times only a limitation and a handicap. Like the time you wanted to go out for a bike ride, and I asked you first, in order to make sure, if you knew which side of the road you had to keep to.

— The right, you answered, as a matter of course.

— Yes, but where is right? I insisted and drew a road on a piece of paper, with our house at one end and the neighbour's at the other. You indicated with your finger which side was right when you cycled toward the neighbour's. Then I told you to turn and cycle back toward our house, and asked where right was now.

— There, you answered, cocksure, and pointed to the same side of the road as before.

But there was something that didn't add up. So far, we'd been sitting looking at the drawing from the side where our house lay. Now we crawled around the paper and looked at the road from the neighbour's house, and when you cycled home this time, right was on the other side.

You despaired. We repeated the experiment by standing face to face and lifting our right arms, then changed places and did the same. Again it was wrong — right changed sides. You became angry and aggrieved.

— Why can't things be the same? Why have they taught me that right is on this side when it isn't true?

You didn't understand, and it made you confused and ashamed, and you went and lay down on the sofa and buried your head in the cushion and didn't want me to see you crying. We've talked about it later several times, but still you have trouble accepting that right can change places according to where you point with your right arm. In one way, I imagine, it's evidence of a kind of humility, as though you don't presume that your arms have the power of decision over something as big as the position of right and left.

It's usually called a paradox when two things that are self-contradictory can be true at the same time. For example, when right can be on both sides of the road. Or when something that feels good and safe can also be painful. If a Norwegian says that all Norwegians lie — is he then telling the truth, or is he lying? Is he perhaps doing both? It seems impossible and confusing, but not even paradoxes are dangerous, they're just yet another thrilling way in which the world can be explained and experienced. Believe me, you yourself are something of a paradox, complex and unpredictable and challenging, never boring, never monotonous, and never easy to fathom. You're simply a whole language, Gabriel.

CHAPTER TEN

*S*ometimes it has already been dark for a long time, sometimes the sun is still riding high in the sky. The house might be empty apart from the two of us and the animals, or it might be full of life and laughter, music and conversation. No matter what, you always have to go to bed, and each evening it seems to you just as unreasonable.

It isn't hard to understand you. For someone with no grasp of clock-time, only of before-and-after time, it cannot be easy to come to terms with the fact that the words "late," "evening," and, "night" should all carry the same merciless implication of

bed and sleep, regardless of whether the summer sky is scintil-
latingly bright or winter darkness has long since fallen, whether
guests are gathered for a party in the living room, or the house is
one big sleepy yawn.

And yet bedtime is each time an occasion for reconciliation.
A day that broke containing every possibility has come to an
end. Most of them came to nothing, and that is an experience
of loss we will go on living with. As a rule, the days resemble
one another to the point of confusion. They are everydays, and
little has happened: the sun has risen, the wind has blown, and
it has been a good day, or not. Even good and bad days can be
hard to distinguish, for they are like all other good and bad
days. And this too, that the everyday days come and go so
anonymously and quietly that we hardly notice them, that they
seem unlived, or lived through as though in a trance, is something we will come to terms with. Moreover, we will manage to
let go of those days that simply want to go on, that refuse to end,
that are so spectacular, so brimming with power and energy
that they splash over into the night with laughter and magic
and joy, or with grief and violence and tears. Even to these we
will not cling.

At bedtime we only cling to each other, not to time, because
we have lost it, it is gone. At bedtime only the body and the certainty of nearness remain, and the promise that nearness gives,
that all is forgiven, and that tomorrow we will not be alone.

WHEN IT'S YOUR BEDTIME and you can choose, because both Mom and I are home, you always give clear instructions about who you want to put you to bed. It's impossible to discover a pattern in your choices, but you are never in doubt. Your decision is final and irrevocable, and only very rarely will you entertain an objection or an alternative solution. Once you have picked Mom, that's final. It doesn't matter that I might want to, or that she might prefer to sit and watch the news in peace. Nor do you see any reason to change your choice if I am the one you have picked, even if I explain that I have a long night's work ahead, whereas Mom actually would like a cuddle with you:

— That's not a problem, Mom can just come up afterwards, when we're finished.

This evening I am the lucky recipient of your favour. Mom and Victoria have had their goodnight hugs, and Balder, who knows what the sight of Gabriel in pajamas means, has sneaked on ahead to claim a place at the foot of the bed.

Stepping inside your room, shutting the world out with the blinds, we also put behind us the day and all that it has been. At bedtime your room is a time capsule, freed from house and calendar, in which we can travel and dream. But first everything must find its proper place.

The reindeer hide has to be over the sheet, and the velvet Siamese pillow with the elephant embroidered in gold has to be next to the ordinary pillow, over which the goatskin is draped.

The golden silk blanket has to be ready so that you can spread it over yourself and sleep with a membrane of China between your body and the duvet. On the shelf above the bed a couple of Buddhas, a conch, a glossy silver money box in the form of horse and a miniature brass canon on wheels have taken up permanent abode. Each evening they are supplemented with a handful of other treasures, and this time it is the turn of the opals and the mother-of-pearls. It takes a long time to find them, especially the ones you hid in the cellar a few days ago and have forgotten where, but which I seem to remember I saw behind the dirty laundry basket, and which — thank God — turns out to be exactly where they are.

Then you have to choose a book. We read to you almost every evening, but never know beforehand which book you want to have read. In these matters too you follow a hidden pattern, or perhaps it's simply whimsical. Whatever, it cannot be taken for granted that you'll wish to continue with the story you heard the beginning of yesterday, especially not if it was Mom who was reading to you. At times it seems as though you choose your books by voice — *Pinocchio* ought to be Mom, *Ronja the Pirate Girl* is best for Dad.

At last we lie down, you on the velvet pillow beneath the oriental silk, me under a crocheted Norwegian quilt with a rolled-up teddy bear to cushion my head. I open the book to begin, but you interrupt at once:

— My heartsticks!

You're referring to the chopsticks of blue, yellow, red, and green plastic, which you collected at cafés and restaurants in Thailand. These are heart-shaped at one end and you have, I believe, forty-six of them. Now you have to get out of bed to make sure that they are lying as they should be lying — on the table, sorted by colour into groups and, not almost but exactly, parallel. They are, but you deliberately dislodge a couple in order to put them back, with immense precision and great satisfaction. It is as though you need to prove to yourself that you are able to restore order to even the most trivial cases of disarray.

You return to bed and make yourself comfortable. It is an ordinary single bed and you are a child, but your body needs room. We are to lie close, but not too close; you want the blanket and the duvet well wrapped around you, but they mustn't be tight, and they will be unless I move even farther out towards the edge. You want to be able to see the book while I'm reading, so my arm on your side has to lie flat, but not between us, because then there won't be enough room. In the end I'm lying with one foot on the floor, the opposing arm twisted up across my chest, with the slightly uncomfortable edge of the bed sticking into my back. But you lie there like a prince, and we can abandon ourselves to the storytelling.

FAIRY TALES AND ADVENTURE stories have the same status for you as playing "let's pretend" — in fact, such stories are even a touch less real, since they're not even a product of your own imagination, in which the categories of reality constantly overflow into one another. Invented stories are like cartoon films, they're funny and odd, they can be exciting and a bit frightening, but you know that they are not *really* real. Moreover, you're secure in the knowledge that you cannot be held responsible for anything that happens in them: they are, so to speak, not your fault, and everything that does not require you relating to it as if you were a part of the chain of cause and effect is a relief to you. Admittedly, this does not prevent you from using scenes from adventure stories as partial arguments in pursuit of some goal, as when you point out that the Indian boys in *Pocahontas* are allowed to carry knives on their own in the forest, so why must you always have a grown-up with you? In cases like this you are, nevertheless, aware of the limited validity of your argument, and give up as soon as we make the point that it doesn't count, that's something you can only do in cartoons.

— Oh yes, I forgot, you hasten to say, even though you haven't forgotten anything at all, but just want to assure us that you know the difference between the pretend and the real.

Books are a different matter. Books can contain fairy tales and adventure stories, but they can also contain descriptions of how, for example, a volcano works, or of which animals live where in the world. Books are, by nature, marred by unreliability, for you cannot know beforehand whether what's in them is true or invented. Is that perhaps even the reason behind your inexplicable aversion to reading them? Because you were in some way afraid to digest information that you had no way of knowing how to handle?

In this respect, books resemble television. You know, because we have said so, that what they show in the news is "true," but you find it difficult to understand the difference when you see a film. After all, the people in a film are living people, so how can you tell when they're actors who are pretending and when they're really just being themselves?

— It isn't dangerous, it's probably just acting, you might say when you see scenes of war on the evening news. A little later it seems just as obvious to you to ask, when you see Tarzan entering a palace in the jungle, whether we can go there too.

The best is if we begin by defining the content of the books we read to you and the films you watch, so that you can tune in to the correct frequency: emotional involvement, for stories that are just pretend; or receptive, for the acquisition of reliable information. Cases where the location of the content is in recognizable, "real" surroundings, but the content itself an invention, pose particular difficulties. You have to deal with the fact that something can be simultaneously real and imaginary. You accept it reluctantly when I compare the situation to those times when you play at being a king who lives in a castle, even though in reality you are Gabriel, and live in a house: you are *both* a pretend king *and* a real Gabriel. Your reluctance proceeds naturally from the fact that there is a logical flaw in the reasoning — play is essentially make-believe, so reality doesn't actually have anything to do with it.

An almost insurmountable trial that initially drove you to the brink of fury arose as we sat one evening and watched an American documentary film — a genre that is, by definition, really real — in which pictures of the New York skyline were shown. There were the Twin Towers in all their majesty, and yet you knew, beyond the shadow of a doubt, that they no longer existed, for on countless occasions, in trustworthy news broadcasts, you had seen them collapse to the ground. In other words, they were *lying* on television, even though I had said that what we were watching was "for real." My simple observation that the film was made before September 11 seemed to you a dubious piece of sophistry, for on television and in books the chronological and therefore conceivable progression of time is abandoned, and the only time you can rely on is the time of your own subjective experience. The order in which you experience events is for you also the actual order of events. And no one was going to try to get you to believe that buildings you had seen explode and crumble to dust long ago could suddenly rise up just as whole and unharmed.

However, this was one problem where you found the solution yourself: I had been mistaken. The documentary was just acting after all.

— But it doesn't matter, Dad. I get it wrong too sometimes when I think something is for real. Let's not talk any more about it.

NOW I LIE HERE and read to you. We have fastened a sky of luminous planets to the ceiling above us, and it is impossible to tell from your eyes whether you are in the forest with Ronja and the pirates, on your way from Saturn to Pluto in a spaceship, or somewhere else completely that I know nothing about. You lie still and silent, and even though I know you're listening, I don't know if what you hear goes directly into storage deep down in your memory or if it first passes through your consciousness for processing.

You always listen and you hear everything, but it often seems as though you simply archive it for later use. Whichever, you very frequently show no noticeable reaction to what is being said. We have gradually learned not always to demand an answer when we talk to you, for there are times when you seem to be storing information without even being aware of the fact yourself. If we ask what you think after we have told you something, you might look at us uncomprehendingly, with apparently no idea of what we are talking about. But later that same day, or after a week, you might suddenly, in a quite different context, pick up the thread and request a more extensive, a better explanation.

Bedtime reading is over for today. I close the book, lay it to one side, and turn off the lamp above your bed. You turn in toward the wall, feel with a hand behind your back just to make certain I'm still there and haven't tried to sneak out of the bed. We lie like this and hear each other exhale at the close of day in the pale green sheen of the solar system above us. After a while, you turn over on your back again, a sure sign that you want to talk.

— Hey, Dad?

— Yes, Gabriel?

— Who's going to look after me when I'm grown up, when you and Mom die and I can't live with you anymore? Because I have to live in my own house when I'm a grown-up. Do you think I'll be completely alone?

These questions pain me where I am most vulnerable, but you ask them in a quiet, sober voice. They convey little more than clinical, sincere curiosity, as though you were inquiring about train times or holiday plans. All the same, it's hard for me to believe in the serenity. I feel something swell in my throat, a

physical response to something inconsolable in you that I sense
you must carry with you always, simply to be able to formulate
such questions.

— No, I don't think you'll be alone, Gabriel. There are so
many people who love you, I say, turning toward you and
stroking your cheek.

You turn too, look straight at me with a look I cannot fathom
in the dim, planetary light, and continue:

— Imagine, perhaps I'll be completely alone when I grow
up, just me and my house when it's time to go to bed, and no
one to look after me! What'll I do then, Dad?

Now it is you who strokes my cheek, as though you sense
that I am the one who needs comfort. My throat has become so
constricted that all I can do is mumble:

— I don't know, son, I don't know.

I DON'T KNOW. It's a pitiful reply to questions that are so
honest and big and important. Pitiful, and yet any other answer
would have been an insult to you, for it would have been a lie.
Mom and I think constantly about what you're going to do the
day you become, in your own way, an adult, the day when we are
no longer there, the day when you are left to fend for yourself.
And we don't know. We watch with great joy how you grow and

become stronger, how you develop abilities and knowledge like any other child, how your personality gradually forms. But we don't know, we cannot know if this will be enough. If you and the world will learn to accept each other, to understand enough of each other to live together in tolerance. We cannot know if you will be completely alone, Gabriel, nor can we know if you will manage to be completely alone.

Your prospects for the future preoccupy you, and every now and then you ask if you will always have your problems — usually with an implicit hope that they will go away and you will one day be "well." At times like that we never lie to you but answer, yes, unfortunately, your problems will be with you all your life, or at least for as long as medical science is unable to cure them.

When I speak of your problems to others, I sometimes compare you to someone who was born without a little finger: it will never grow, and the person affected must spend his whole life with only nine fingers. But, I hasten to add, that doesn't mean that a person like that can never become an outstanding concert pianist or a surgeon, with sufficient help and practice. Life must simply be adjusted to allow for the absence of this one finger. In the same way you will have to accept that your problems will be with you for the rest of your life. That does not mean — far from it — that you will continue to be a troubled child. To the contrary: your body, your intelligence, and your sensibilities will mature and develop, and you will turn into a grown man with many possibilities. If you are given help along the way, and in addition learn to help yourself, there is no reason why you shouldn't live a long and good and rich life.

— I WANT TO GET MARRIED when I grow up, you say.

Is that because you are a child and want to live an adult life in the only way you know of, together with someone you love, like Mom and I? Is that all? Or do you already know, intuitively, without understanding what it is you know, that you will need someone, that it will be too difficult alone? Is it a practical solution to a practical problem you are envisioning? Is that why you add, as though you needed an instruction manual:

— But how will I be able to get married when I'm grown up?

— Don't worry about that now. There's a long time to go before you're big enough to decide whether you want to get married.

The truth is, I try to talk the whole problem away. I try to push it into the future, as if a better answer lay waiting there. The truth is that I fear the question because I don't believe it has a happy answer, and because it therefore nourishes a deep grief. The truth is I don't know if you will ever marry, Gabriel, and have a family of your own. Love between adults is the most complex relationship that exists. It demands so much of all that you do not have and do not understand, of a language that is often ambiguous and unspoken and implied, of such a deeply empathic acceptance of another human that at times it feels like losing oneself. You, who fumbles so with the idea of your own self, who struggles to understand that other people have another self, and that you must relinquish a little of yours and accept a little of theirs in order to establish even the most superficial social relationships — will you be able to live in community and in marriage?

Sorrow and uncertainty and the urge to be sincere fight for possession of me, filling the moment with a gravity I cannot find a way out of. But you can.

— Dad, do you think I can take my treasures to my girlfriend when I'm grown up?

It is said in the same sober, wondering tone of voice, but for me it's the best line of the day. Suddenly, all is harmless laughter and joking again: but of course you'll take your treasures with you, all of them! Only an obstinate clot of memory lodged in my throat tells me that this is not over; this will never be over.

THE GREEN SHEEN OF LIGHT from the ceiling is slowly dwindling, the planets are about to go out. You don't like the darkness, and I know that as soon as I have gone downstairs you'll switch on the light above the bed, even though the door to the lit hallway is wide open. If you've fallen asleep before I go, at some point in the course of the night you'll register the darkness, and a hand in search of renewed security will find the switch.

Right now my body is all the safety you need. You lie on your side, turned toward the wall as usual, with me as a shield against the world at your back. I sing "The earth is lovely" for you, very quietly, almost pure breathing, as I have done ever since you were very small. No doubt you think the psalm is pretty, but it is the repetition that calms you, that tells you that all is well because all is as it usually is.

From the corner of my eye I see Mom in the doorway watching us. She comes over to the bed, bends carefully over me, and kisses you on the cheek. You are too tired, you're lying too comfortably to turn over and look at her, but as if from somewhere else we hear your voice:

— When I die and go to heaven, can we cuddle a bit more then?

We say nothing, but rest smiling hands on your head. What a fantastic boy, our eyes say to each other.

At bedtimes like these, at moments of grace like these, all

has been overcome, all has been understood. Everything is a miracle. You are Gabriel and the whole world is your treasure chamber.

Sleep tight, my son. Tomorrow we'll live on.

EPILOGUE

From: **dad@frometoyou.no**
To: **gabriel@frometoyou.no**
Subject: **Greetings from New York**

Dear Gabriel:

I'm sitting on a bench in New York City. If the Atlantic Ocean weren't so enormous we could have waved to each other — you from our garden back home and me from one of the sky-scrapers that surrounds the park I'm sitting in.

Even though I know quite a few people in this city, I have to

confess I feel quite lonely here. I see the people around me living their daily lives, and I sense more strongly than in other
places that here I am only a visitor. Something about all the
hurry, I imagine. Their daily life isn't mine, and probably
never could be. Not that most people aren't nice and don't
do their best to make me feel at home, but somehow it
doesn't help. Sometimes their friendliness actually makes it
more difficult: the more they try to make me feel welcome,
the more obvious it is that I don't belong here, that I am
not a part of their reality.

I've had similar experiences many times before, when passing through realities that aren't mine. And each time that happens, I think about how much more common and challenging
such experiences are for you, how you struggle to feel at home
even when you are at home or at school or in a shop or with
friends — in those realities which by every standard must be
called your own. And for the umpteenth time I ask myself:
What does it really mean to feel at home in your own reality?

I still don't have a good answer for you. In fact, in many
ways I feel as though the answer slips away and becomes more
elusive each time I ask: What is my reality? Where do I
belong?

Perhaps I should simply stop asking. Perhaps it's the question itself, this ceaseless and restless wondering, that prevents
my feeling of alienation from ever ending. If we just stopped

asking ourselves such questions, would everything fall into place? Would we find our place and resign ourselves to it, find contentment in it?

Forgive me. I know that difficult questions about the meaning of life aren't what you want and expect from your father when he sends you greetings from New York. What you'd probably like best is for me to put the computer away and spend time buying cool clothes for you. And I promise I will; I'll come back home with something you want. But first, let me tell you that, the way I see it, these questions are among your gifts to me. If it weren't for you I wouldn't have asked them to begin with, or at least not given them as much thought as I have. And believe me, son, I wouldn't want to be without them. The sense of wonder you've given rise to is, at heart, the reality in which I feel most at home. Perhaps — but this is only a guess — because it ties me so closely to you.

You probably won't remember, because you were so little at the time, but several years ago you and I passed through New York. You were perhaps two or three, and we didn't know much about you other than that you were a beautiful miracle, bursting with life. It was in the days when the Twin Towers still stood and reached up into the skies before they were struck and fell.

It was also before Mom and I knew that you had already been struck in your own way, and that you would fall all too easily when the world came charging at you with all its requests and demands, and you didn't have enough strength and resistance to stay upright. Or rather — you had more than enough strength. What you lacked was the understanding of when to use it, and in what way, and how much. And so you fell, because you were confused and distressed and paralyzed in the face of a world that seemed constantly to attack you.

Now you're turning into a tall, splendid young man, and this time we're here together in another way: a literary festival that features writers from all over the world has invited me to talk about you and to read from this book. But I'll tell you: it isn't that easy, even though I'm the one who wrote the book and even though it's about you, my son. Quite simply because the boy I was writing about no longer exists.

Time moves on, even for a boy described in a book. The years have matured him; he has developed intellectually and emotionally, and not least physically. He has acquired new interests, and encountered new challenges. The boy has turned into a young man. And so while I wait here, backstage — perhaps no more than ten minutes after we've spoken on the phone because you called to ask permission to stay the night at a friend's house, having forgotten that I'm away — I have to remind myself that the public out there is expecting to hear about the person you were, not the person you are.

Like any other parent, I always think of you as I see you, developing day by day. But many people who know you first and foremost through the description of your problems seem almost to expect you to have stood still, to forever remain that lovely little boy who struggles to understand the world and to be understood by it. Or they assume that all those problems you've contended with must surely be resolved by now. You wouldn't believe the number of times I've heard something along the lines of:

— Ah yes, aren't you the one who had the son with all the difficulties? How's he doing? Is everything okay now?

In both cases people seem to hope for the simplest possible answer — either that nothing has happened, and they can go on relating to you as though you were still that sweet, charming but heartbreaking Gabriel, or that you've "grown out of" your problems since the last time they heard about you.

But, of course, it isn't like that. Simple answers are usually a product of wishful thinking. No one knows that better than you, having spent your whole life wishing you had another life.

Now I'm standing with some other writers in a lecture hall near the big park that lies in the centre of this "Big Apple," as the

Americans call their great city, the one you once took a tiny bite from. We are each going to say a few words and then read from our books. The others are well-known French and American writers, and I begin to doubt whether my little story about you will be of much interest to the two or three hundred people sitting here. Feeling nervous, I let my thoughts wander to more pragmatic questions.

I hope the sleepover goes okay and that Henni has remembered to give him money for Cokes and pizza, I think as the moderator opens the program and invites the first guest, a bestselling American writer of historical novels about love and war, onto the stage. *And that he doesn't let himself be tricked into spending it all on treating his friends*.

Your friendships are still so new you're willing to do anything to hang onto your recently acquired pals. Unfortunately, I sometimes suspect them of exploiting your keenness by, among other things, spending all your money. You are by nature wonderfully generous and unselfish, and if your kindness can also win friends for you then you're quite willing to give away all you've got. Even though you've seen, on a number of occasions, so-called friends turn their backs on you the moment you have no more left to give.

I feel anger flaring up in me at the mere thought, and the urge to interfere long-distance from New York is kept in check only by a reluctant admonishment to myself that this is something Gabriel has to deal with on his own, this is something he's going to have to go through and experience without help, this is something he has to learn to handle — just like every other young man. Even though you aren't always like all the other young men, you've got to drill it into yourself to be like them, for you will — you will and you must! — learn to manage on your own.

Remember how many times I've said that to you? How often Mom and I have drummed into you that you must keep trying and never give up? Because the world takes no special account of you, dear Gabriel, any more than it does any other individual. It is you who must learn to accommodate yourself to the world, to distinguish between the happy times when it wishes you well, and the all-too-frequent occasions when it mows you down, uninterested, cynical, and unscrupulous. And if you ask me how to learn to tell the difference — well, I'll have to send the question right back at you. Because at the heart of it lies a riddle: How is it possible to hold on to the good in yourself, when what the world seems to reward is the bad? It's a riddle that three thousand years of philosophical and religious discussion has failed to solve — unless, perhaps, the solution lies in the act of questioning itself.

❧

Ha! That's easy for me to say, I think, as a salvo of thunderous applause greets the popular, bestselling author, who has just concluded a reading from his most recent and highly controversial novel about homosexual love during the American Civil War. *What if, at the deepest level, he has already conceded defeat? What if he's just playing along so as not to disappoint us?*

Over the years you've grown disturbingly good at pretending, Gabriel. What used to be one of your foremost characteristics, your inability to dissemble or lie, you've gradually turned around and developed into something I suppose is a kind of survival strategy. The same world that ceaselessly charges at you with demands and expectations that seem so impossible to meet also offers you a wide and tempting range of potential solutions. Everywhere you turn you encounter apparently approved patterns of behavior that promise you all will be well, if only you make them your own and fashion yourself after them. Clothes, language, pastimes, attitudes, opinions — the world is rife with ready-made behavioral patterns, just help yourself. On top of that, popular culture's incessant cultivation of intoxicants and states of intoxication offers you the best excuse to indulge in self-medication disguised as self-realization.

For most young people, all of this is a supermarket of identities from which they can freely pick and choose and combine in whatever way suits their personal preferences and dispositions. But for you it is much more than that: to you they seem like existential escape routes, short-cuts you can take to be like the others, to stop lacking what you believe the others have — to simply stop being Gabriel. And even though you probably suspect that this must be a fundamental impossibility, you try to achieve it in the only way you know how: by pretending.

That frightens me, I have to tell you. Dissimulation is just a pretty word for lying, and lying is a swamp that sucks all life and swallows it down, leaving nothing behind but darkness, emptiness, and fear. At the same time I understand you so well, and I wish I could support you in this effort too. But, my dearest boy, I cannot help you become someone other than who you are. That would imply betraying you, as fundamentally as a lie betrays. And it would be a betrayal of myself. I can only try to help you come to terms with the fact that you are Gabriel — unique, irreplaceable Gabriel.

Now, a surprisingly young French poet takes the stage. I would guess she's about your age, clearly a precocious lyrical talent, but I can't quite grasp her poetical intentions. This is not only due to her French way of lisping and burring her recitation of the English translation, but also because the slight and charmless figure I see in profile from my place in the wings radiates a singular absence which reminds me of you.

I know nothing about this young lady apart from the fact that, according to our moderator, she has already managed to publish a collection of poetry that has been highly praised by influential Parisian critics. But I have no problem imagining that the poetical cornucopia from which she seems to draw so effortlessly and playfully occupies much of the space that is, in others, set aside for the experiences of life. *She must be extremely boring*, I think to myself, *the moment she leaves her keyboard and her poetical universe*. Of course, I might be wrong, I might just be prejudiced. But still, in the life I imagine she's chosen not to live I seem to recognize your longing, your insatiable thirst for all those experiences that you imagine a life in full demands of you.

Of course a lot of it is about girls and sex and love, and why shouldn't it be? In this respect you're no different from all the other young people feeling their way forward, as terrified as they are aroused by the mysteries of love and of sensual pleasure. But whereas most are more or less open to the randomness of these encounters, ready to follow an attraction wherever it may lead them, there are times when it seems as though you operate with a mental form, ticking off experiences as you complete them.

My heart is in my mouth as I write this, Gabriel, because I would hate for you to misunderstand me. There is nothing wrong with the way you go in search of love and girlfriends. To the contrary, the point is precisely that in this field there are no rules, nor any sets of instructions. I know you are painfully aware that social relationships between people are guided by complex and unwritten laws, which seem impossible to learn. But you mustn't let this tempt you into believing that guidelines exist for what and how and how much you should feel. If you hear your friends describing, or perhaps even boasting of, the way in which they've done "it," you mustn't believe that they're talking about some universal formula that you too should apply. No one chooses their feelings — that's something you should know better than most, as vulnerable to them as you are.

However, we are to a large extent responsible for the actions our emotions give rise to, and in these choices it might be a good idea to observe certain basic rules. But I really don't have to tell you about this either. You've had enough experience dealing with the consequences of letting your feelings take control, of acting on impulse because you were happy or angry or proud or sad — or some confusing mixture of all. And you have most definitely experienced the unfairness of others doing the same to you. How I have admired you all those times you've been the subject of gross abuse, come home with huge bruises on your arms and shoulders because bullies at school thought they could impress girls by beating you up, or met your pals at the mall only to be mocked and humiliated because their insecurity made them afraid to acknowledge you — the list is as long as it is painful. But each time it's happened, you've let it pass, given them another chance, and shrugged off the degradation and the insult with a brave smile, even though you didn't understand why they treated you so cruelly.

It may well be admirable to bear the weight of literary fame at an early age, as the girl on stage is doing now, responding with studied self-assurance to the audience's enthusiastic bravissimos. But if you ask me, that's nothing compared to the unflinching way you carry your life, each and every day, and all too often at the risk of being booed off the stage.

Now I hear our names, and it feels as if we're being summoned from the playground to the principal's office because we've done something wrong and are about to be reprimanded. Naturally, I'm nervous and tense. It's one thing to sit hidden behind a screen and write about you, but to stand exposed on stage and talk about you — about us?

Yes, dammit! If you can do it, then I can do it too. And what's more, it's you I'm talking to; this is all about you. So listen:

I start with a few words about your problems, what typifies them, and what it was like to be told by the doctors that our son was born with certain difficulties he would have to struggle with all his life, but for which they — the doctors — unfortunately couldn't give us any real explanation. They couldn't say anything definite about the causes of the problems, and they were uncertain about the degree of hardships we might expect them to cause you. The only thing they were certain about was that your problems had a name, and so they gave you a so-called diagnosis.

Naturally it came as a shock, perhaps less for Mom, who suspected something was wrong, than it was for me. It was as though I refused to believe there could be anything wrong with my son. Instead I comforted myself with the thought that you would develop at your own pace and in your own time, and that all would work out in the end. It was, I told myself, just a question of being patient, of letting time and maturity work for you. But then we got the diagnosis, and there was no longer any point in protesting.

A diagnosis. You have no idea how many times I've twisted and turned that word around in my head, trying to come to terms with what it means, what it implies for you and for us, your family. And I have come to think that with a problem as deep-seated and pervasive as yours, the diagnosis itself can in many ways be compared to having a grave to visit for a mother or father who has lost a child.

This may sound extreme, almost brutal. But all I mean to say is that there's a certainty there, a kind of clarification; a grave is a concrete place to go to with one's grief and one's loss. However, a grave doesn't have much more to offer than that. It cannot give the child back to his or her parents, no more than it can explain why this awful thing has happened, nor how to learn to live with it.

In that sense it's similar to your diagnosis: It solves nothing. It can't help you be like the others, and it doesn't explain which connections in your neurobiological circuitry are functioning in a different way; nor why you, and not someone else, have been afflicted; nor what we can do to help you and ourselves to live with your problems.

Then what use is it? You have a perfect right to ask.

I'm sorry, son, but again, I'm at a loss to answer you. The only way you can use the diagnosis is to identify your problems. It won't make them go away. It will just give them a name to use when you talk about them, a name that will, hopefully, help other people understand why you are the way you are.

We've talked about this before, how names can be important. Names are what keep the world in order when we talk to each other about it. Names are what enable us to know what we're talking about.

Many years ago you explained this to me yourself in your own way. You must have been about ten or twelve years old, an age when you thought you knew all you needed to know about what a real Indian was. You came up to me with an unusual glint in your eyes and asked:

— Hey Dad, if you had a friend who was a real Indian, would you call him up once in a while to find out how he was?

I, who in my innocence thought that you were investigating the extent of my kind-heartedness, at once replied that if the Indian were a good friend of mine, then of course I would call him up from time to time to make sure he was all right.

At that you grinned hugely, certain that on this occasion you had the verbal advantage over me, a practical understanding of the significance of a name.

— No, you said. Because if your friend had been a real Indian, then he wouldn't have had a telephone!

This little story of yours raises a chuckle in the audience. I use the interlude to wind up my introduction with a few words about why I wrote this book to you, and why I wrote it the way I did, in the form of a long letter.

It was, I say, first and foremost because I had to find a form that did not compromise you, a form that would enable me to look you in the eye — and myself in the mirror — when the time came for you to read what I had written. I wanted there to be no reason for you to feel misunderstood or exposed or betrayed, and therefore I had to be on guard against anything that might seem hurtful or sensational or improper or vulgar. I also needed to find a form that compelled me to be open, honest, and — to the extent it might be necessary — to reveal unpleasant sides of myself as well. I had to avoid prettifying or idealizing the situation. That, it seemed to me, would be tantamount to not taking you, your problems, or myself seriously. Another form of betrayal.

I spent a long time experimenting with different ways of doing it, but nothing worked until I finally decided to write you a letter. When a father writes a letter to his son, I thought, a letter that will also be read by others, strangers, then he cannot permit himself to write hurtfully or superficially or poorly. Whether or not I have succeeded, in the final analysis only you can be the judge of that.

Now it's time to read an extract. This is the part I have dreaded the most, even though I've done it many times before, because it always feels oddly private to be sharing my thoughts about you, and to you, with others.

At the same time — and without it seeming the least bit contradictory — I look forward to it, because when I stand in front of the microphone with the book in my hand and look down at the sentences I have written (though in fact I know most of them practically off by heart), you appear before me so clearly it's as though we're standing there together.

I open the book to the page I've decided to read from, and in my mind I reach out a hand and take yours. I feel the security and encouragement that flows from you, and so I begin.

Afterwards, I close the book and thank the audience for listening. The room remains silent for a disquietingly long time. Then the applause comes, but it seems strangely reserved, not as enthusiastic as I had hoped.

The moderator replaces me at the microphone and rather hesitantly announces that the next and final guest really needs no introduction. She is a revered grand old lady of American letters, and without a doubt the main attraction for the audience.

The silence in the room is palpable as she strides onto the stage. She stands there with a few sheets of paper in her hand and seems to draw out the silence, as if unsure what to do. And then she pays us — you and me, Gabriel — the greatest compliment I can imagine. She stares down at her manuscript for a long time before setting it down, then lifts her gaze towards the room and says firmly:

— You know what? I think we should all just go out into the park and think about things for a while.

And that's where I'm sitting now, on a bench in the park, finishing off this email to you that has turned out to be so much longer than I intended. But it's late evening here, and therefore early morning where you are, so you should have plenty of time to read it.

Have a good day, son. Talk to you soon.

Big hug from Dad.

AFTERWORD

$\mathcal{T}$he "problems" that are referred to in this book have been diagnosed respectively as *atypical autism* and *ADHD*.

Autism (from the Greek *auto*, meaning "one self") is a so-called pervasive developmental disorder. It is called "pervasive" because it affects crucial functions such as the ability to communicate and to understand interaction with others, and because it affects behaviour in all contexts and situations. We don't know the exact cause, but scientists agree that autism results from an abnormal development in the nervous system that causes certain brain activities to develop in a different way than they do in most people. Although more than sixty years have passed since the American psychiatrist Leo Kanner first used the term *autism* as an independent diagnosis for people suffering from such a developmental disorder, no one has yet been able to explain why and how it arises — although some theories seem more plausible than others. Furthermore, many will argue that the children who meet the criteria for autism are so different from one another in their development and manners that it would seem unreasonable to suggest that their conditions have a single common cause. There are probably several different causes for their functional disorders, and the causes may vary from child to child. Many autistic children (up to seventy percent) also have a milder or more serious mental disability.

Even if the causes of autism remain largely unknown, we now know a great deal about its most important features. Autism is basically a lack of ability to understand social relations and interaction. A scientist has put it this way: "Autism is [among other things] not being able to imagine that oneself and one or several other persons are talking about the same thing. Therefore much of the social world is perceived as unpredictable and thereby frightening." The American Academy of Science has said that autism "affects basic human behavior such as social interaction, the ability to express thoughts and feelings, imagination and the establishment of relationships with others."

The specific diagnosis of "atypical autism" is made in cases where there is a lack of sufficiently established criteria to comply with the alternative, which is "infantile autism." For example, the criterion of "stereotyped, repetitive behavior" might not be found, and therefore the diagnosis cannot be sufficiently proven.

There is agreement that autistic persons have serious difficulties with social interaction because they somehow lack the ability to understand what others say and do, and why. Autistic persons are not able to empathize with other people's thoughts and conceptions, or to appreciate the value of doing so. They therefore have a serious challenge in all social contexts: if two or more individuals are to participate equally in a school class, a game, or a conversation on the street, it is an important condition that they, at least then and there, have a common understanding of the situation in which they are participating. Should one of them lack such an understanding, he or she would be like the one blind person in a group of friends who are conversing about a sculpture. While the others discuss the colour and shape of the figure in front of them, the blind one will have to be content with talking about the impression he or she has gathered from touching it. How can the individual understand what the others are saying, and how can the others understand the individual? Both parties may as well be talking about two different sculptures.

Another way of putting it, when explaining autism to children, is asking them to imagine that a Canadian boy travelled in a time machine to a small Chinese village two hundred years ago. He won't understand what the Chinese are saying to one another or to him, and they won't have a clue what he is saying in return. This last part is important, because an autistic person has a twofold problem: he doesn't always understand what other people are saying or doing, and in addition, he himself is easily misunderstood because others don't often consider that he doesn't get what they say and do. Instead, the others may accuse him of being less intellectually endowed than they.

But autism has nothing to do with intellectual capability. Among autistic persons there are, just as among everyone else, geniuses and individuals with severe intellectual impairments. Furthermore, the diagnosis spans those who are so severely afflicted that they completely lack language and others who have only mild autistic features and might seem indistinguishable in their behaviour from those who function normally. Scientists therefore use the term *the autism spectrum* to suggest how great the differences are between the various forms and degrees of autism.

Many books and movies give the impression that autistic people surely have their problems, but that on the other hand they are idiot savants, "wise idiots," all of them ostensibly equipped with rare and somehow inexplicable gifts in fields such as music, mathematics, or astronomy. This is a myth that contributes to the mystification of a condition that is mysterious enough as it is — although it is correct that many autistic persons become unusually passionate about a specific activity and cultivate specific talents.

When autism was first made an issue, many thought that children were afflicted because they had cold and distant mothers. The vast majority of scientists now view this as being completely wrong. Instead, they have tried to chart the basic features of autism and to create explanatory models of how the disorders develop.

In several books written by autistic persons it is more or less explicitly implied that autism can be "cured." This is not true, and such suggestions are dangerous in that they lead parents to have unrealistic expectations when they should be concentrating on helping their children. These writers are right to say that it is possible to learn and train oneself to live with one's autism in a way that is less detrimental to one's life. An experienced scientist puts it this way: "Autism is a lifelong disorder which might lighten some with age, partly because certain mechanisms may start functioning after a long delay, and therefore are not permanently damaged." For one thing, surveys show that preschool-aged children who appear severely autistic may show much milder symptoms in their youth and as adults. Still, not even such an "improvement" is within a realistic range for many autistic people, who have such grave difficulties that they will never live approximately normal lives. On the other hand, people with severe autism and developmental impairment might be able to establish contact with their surroundings, provided that they are given necessary help and encouragement.

ADHD stands for Attention Deficit Hyperactivity Disorder. People with ADHD have problems with concentrating their attention on one issue over time, and they are full of bodily restlessness — what is often called "hyperactivity." In addition, ADHD often causes anger and aggression, and can lead to thoughtless, impulsive actions. ADHD is, like autism, the result of neurological failure or damage, but is unrelated to intellectual capacity.

Only a very few who have a diagnosis within the autism spectrum also have an ADHD diagnosis. The way diagnostic criteria are formulated, an autism diagnosis would exclude ADHD, even though clinical practice shows that many autistic persons also have problems that are associated with ADHD. But despite the frequent overlapping of the two groups, ADHD is not considered a part of the autism spectrum.

Recent studies suggest that there are up to sixty people afflicted by autism per ten thousand. That means that there could be more than two hundred thousand autistic persons in Canada and over ten million worldwide.

The figures for ADHD patients are even higher. Five to six percent of the population is believed to be affected, that is to say, as many as two million Canadians. Or more precisely: two million unique, exceptional, and singular individuals.

For more information about autism and the autism spectrum:

AUTISM SOCIETY OF CANADA (nationwide chapters)
Represents the largest collective voice of the autism community in Canada. The provincial and territorial autism societies and their member groups in each region provide direct support to people with ASDs (Autism Spectrum Disorders) and their families.

> 1670 Heron Road
> Box 22017
> Ottawa, Ontario K1V 0C2
> www.autismsocietycanada.ca

AUTISM TREATMENT SERVICES OF CANADA
A national affiliation of organizations that provide, or are actively planning to provide, treatment, educational, management, and consultative services to people with autism and related disorders across Canada.

> 404 – 94th Ave. SE
> Calgary, Alberta T2J 0E8
> www.autism.ca

GENEVA CENTRE FOR AUTISM
Committed to providing resources for parents, professionals, and those who are affected by Autism Spectrum Disorders.

> 112 Merton Street
> Toronto, Ontario M4S 2Z8
> www.autism.net

ABOUT THE AUTHOR

*H*alfdan W. Freihow grew up in Mexico, Norway, Spain, and Belgium, and has worked as a publisher, journalist, translator, and literary critic.